Presented to: _____

By: _____

God's Promises® for Singles

NASHVILLE

A Thomas Nelson Company

ISBN: 08499-5675-7

Printed in the United States of America

www.jcountryman.com

Contents

Promises When You Need . . .

Promises About Your Personal Relationships

Promises When You Feel . . .

Promises When You Are . . .

Promises that Jesus Is Your . . .

Promises of Truth from God's Word

Promises About Christian Growth

Promises to Help You Serve God

God's Plan of Salvation . . .

Promises When
You Need . . .

Courage ✈

Wait on the LORD;
Be of good courage,
And He shall strengthen your heart;
Wait, I say, on the LORD!

Psalm 27:14

Beloved, do not think it strange concerning the fiery trial which is to try you, as though some strange thing happened to you; but rejoice to the extent that you partake of Christ's sufferings, that when His glory is revealed, you may also be glad with exceeding joy.

1 Peter 4:12, 13

I am persuaded that neither death nor life, nor angels nor principalities nor powers, nor things present nor things to come, nor height nor depth, nor any other created thing, shall be able to separate us from the love of God which is in Christ Jesus our Lord.

Romans 8:38, 39

Fear not, for I am with you;
Be not dismayed, for I am your God.
I will strengthen you,
Yes, I will help you,
I will uphold you with My righteous right
     hand.

Isaiah 41:10

The eternal God is your refuge, and underneath are the everlasting arms; He will thrust out the enemy from before you, and will say, "Destroy!"

Deuteronomy 33:27

I shall not die, but live, and declare the works of the LORD.

Psalm 118:17

I can do all things through Christ who strengthens me.

Philippians 4:13

Be of good courage, and He shall strengthen your heart, all you who hope in the LORD.

Psalm 31:24

Those who wait on the LORD
Shall renew their strength;
They shall mount up with wings
    like eagles,
They shall run and not be weary,
They shall walk and not faint.

Isaiah 40:31

So the ransomed of the LORD shall return,
And come to Zion with singing,
With everlasting joy on their heads.
They shall obtain joy and gladness;
Sorrow and sighing shall flee away.

Isaiah 51:11

Patience 🕊

But the fruit of the Spirit is love, joy, peace, longsuffering, kindness, goodness, faithfulness.

Galatians 5:22

Knowing that the testing of your faith produces patience.

But let patience have its perfect work, that you may be perfect and complete, lacking nothing.

James 1:3, 4

Do not become sluggish, but imitate those who through faith and patience inherit the promises.

Hebrews 6:12

It is good that one should hope and wait quietly for the salvation of the LORD.

Lamentations 3:26

If we hope for what we do not see, we eagerly wait for it with perseverance.

Romans 8:25

The end of a thing is better than its
      beginning;
The patient in spirit is better than the
      proud in spirit.
Do not hasten in your spirit to be angry,
For anger rests in the bosom of fools.

Ecclesiastes 7:8, 9

Whatever things were written before were
written for our learning, that we through the patience and comfort of the Scriptures might have
hope.

Now may the God of patience and comfort
grant you to be like-minded toward one another,
according to Christ Jesus.

Romans 15:4, 5

Rest in the LORD, and wait patiently for
      Him;
Do not fret because of him who prospers in
      his way,
Because of the man who brings wicked
      schemes to pass.

Psalm 37:7

I waited patiently for the LORD; and He
inclined to me, and heard my cry.

Psalm 40:1

Do not cast away your confidence, which has great reward.

For you have need of endurance, so that after you have done the will of God, you may receive the promise: "For yet a little while, and He who is coming will come and will not tarry."

Hebrews 10:35–37

Since we are surrounded by so great a cloud of witnesses, let us lay aside every weight, and the sin which so easily ensnares us, and let us run with endurance the race that is set before us.

Hebrews 12:1

We also glory in tribulations, knowing that tribulation produces perseverance; and perseverance, character; and character, hope.

Now hope does not disappoint, because the love of God has been poured out in our hearts by the Holy Spirit who was given to us.

Romans 5:3–5

Peace ✐

You will keep him in perfect peace, whose mind is stayed on You, because he trusts in You.

Isaiah 26:3

Be anxious for nothing, but in everything by prayer and supplication, with thanksgiving, let your requests be made known to God; and the peace of God, which surpasses all understanding, will guard your hearts and minds through Christ Jesus.

Philippians 4:6, 7

LORD, You will establish peace for us, for You have also done all our works in us.

Isaiah 26:12

He shall enter into peace; they shall rest in their beds, each one walking in his uprightness.

Isaiah 57:2

You shall go out with joy,
And be led out with peace;
The mountains and the hills
Shall break forth into singing before you,
And all the trees of the field shall clap
    their hands.

Isaiah 55:12

Mark the blameless man, and observe the upright; for the future of that man is peace.

Psalm 37:37

To be carnally minded is death, but to be spiritually minded is life and peace.

Romans 8:6

The kingdom of God is not eating and drinking, but righteousness and peace and joy in the Holy Spirit.

For he who serves Christ in these things is acceptable to God and approved by men.

Therefore let us pursue the things which make for peace and the things by which one may edify another.

Romans 14:17–19

Great peace have those who love Your law, and nothing causes them to stumble.

Psalm 119:165

The meek shall inherit the earth, and shall delight themselves in the abundance of peace.

Psalm 37:11

Finally, brethren, farewell. Become complete. Be of good comfort, be of one mind, live in peace; and the God of love and peace will be with you.

2 Corinthians 13:11

May the God of hope fill you with all joy and peace in believing, that you may abound in hope by the power of the Holy Spirit.

Romans 15:13

Peace I leave with you, My peace I give to you; not as the world gives do I give to you. Let not your heart be troubled, neither let it be afraid.

John 14:27

May the Lord of peace Himself give you peace always in every way.

2 Thessalonians 3:16

Comfort 🕊

I do not want you to be ignorant, brethren, concerning those who have fallen asleep, lest you sorrow as others who have no hope.

For if we believe that Jesus died and rose again, even so God will bring with Him those who sleep in Jesus.

1 Thessalonians 4:13, 14

The LORD has comforted His people, and will have mercy on His afflicted.

Isaiah 49:13b

Blessed are those who mourn, for they shall be comforted.

Matthew 5:4

Blessed be the God and Father of our Lord Jesus Christ, the Father of mercies and God of all comfort, who comforts us in all our tribulation, that we may be able to comfort those who are in any trouble, with the comfort with which we ourselves are comforted by God.

2 Corinthians 1:3, 4

This is my comfort in my affliction, for Your word has given me life.

Psalm 119:50

O Death, where is your sting? O Hades,
    where is your victory?
The sting of death is sin, and the strength
    of sin is the law.
But thanks be to God, who gives us the
    victory through our Lord Jesus Christ.

1 Corinthians 15:55–57

Yea, though I walk through the valley of
    the shadow of death,
I will fear no evil;
For You are with me;
Your rod and Your staff, they comfort me.

Psalm 23:4

God will wipe away every tear from their
eyes; there shall be no more death, nor sorrow,
nor crying. There shall be no more pain, for the
former things have passed away.

Revelation 21:4

Casting all your care upon Him, for He
cares for you.

1 Peter 5:7

Fear not, for I am with you;
Be not dismayed, for I am your God.
I will strengthen you,
Yes, I will help you,
I will uphold you with My righteous
      right hand.

Isaiah 41:10

Behold, I am the LORD, the God of all flesh.
Is there anything too hard for Me?

Jeremiah 32:27

For the eyes of the LORD are on
      the righteous,
And His ears are open to their prayers;
But the face of the LORD is against those
      who do evil.
And who is he who will harm you if you
      become followers of what is good?

1 Peter 3:12–13

Assurance ✒

Jesus answered and said to them, "Have faith in God.

"For assuredly, I say to you, whoever says to this mountain, 'Be removed and be cast into the sea,' and does not doubt in his heart, but believes that those things he says will be done, he will have whatever he says.

"Therefore I say to you, whatever things you ask when you pray, believe that you receive them, and you will have them."

Mark 11:22–24

Do not seek what you should eat or what you should drink, nor have an anxious mind.

For all these things the nations of the world seek after, and your Father knows that you need these things.

But seek the kingdom of God, and all these things shall be added to you.

Luke 12:29–31

He who calls you is faithful, who also will do it.

1 Thessalonians 5:24

He did not waver at the promise of God through unbelief, but was strengthened in faith, giving glory to God, and being fully convinced that what He had promised He was also able to perform.

Romans 4:20, 21

My counsel shall stand,
And I will do all My pleasure . . .
Indeed I have spoken it;
I will also bring it to pass.
I have purposed it;
I will also do it.

Isaiah 46:10b, 11b

The Lord is not slack concerning His promise, as some count slackness, but is longsuffering toward us, not willing that any should perish but that all should come to repentance.

2 Peter 3:9

As for God, His way is perfect; the word of the LORD is proven; He is a shield to all who trust in Him.

Psalm 18:30

The LORD's hand is not shortened, that it cannot save; nor His ear heavy, that it cannot hear.

Isaiah 59:1

Beloved, do not think it strange concerning the fiery trial which is to try you, as though some strange thing happened to you; but rejoice to the extent that you partake of Christ's sufferings, that when His glory is revealed, you may also be glad with exceeding joy.

1 Peter 4:12, 13

For as the rain comes down, and the snow
    from heaven,
And do not return there,
But water the earth,
And make it bring forth and bud,
That it may give seed to the sower
And bread to the eater,
So shall My word be that goes forth from
    My mouth;
It shall not return to Me void,
But it shall accomplish what I please,
And it shall prosper in the thing for which
    I sent it.

Isaiah 55:10, 11

Confidence ✐

I can do all things through Christ who strengthens me.

Philippians 4:13

So we may boldly say: "The LORD is my helper; I will not fear. What can man do to me?"
Hebrews 13:6

Do not cast away your confidence, which has great reward.

For you have need of endurance, so that after you have done the will of God, you may receive the promise.

Hebrews 10:35, 36

Being confident of this very thing, that He who has begun a good work in you will complete it until the day of Jesus Christ.

Philippians 1:6

The LORD God is my strength; He will make my feet like deer's feet, and He will make me walk on my high hills.

Habakkuk 3:19

In all these things we are more than conquerors through Him who loved us.

Romans 8:37

Now this is the confidence that we have in Him, that if we ask anything according to His will, He hears us.

And if we know that He hears us, whatever we ask, we know that we have the petitions that we have asked of Him.

1 John 5:14, 15

Most assuredly, I say to you, he who believes in Me, the works that I do he will do also; and greater works than these he will do, because I go to My Father.

John 14:12

When you pass through the waters, I will
    be with you;
And through the rivers, they shall not
    overflow you.
When you walk through the fire, you shall
    not be burned,
Nor shall the flame scorch you.

Isaiah 43:2

The LORD will be your confidence, and will keep your foot from being caught.

Proverbs 3:26

So he answered and said to me:
"This is the word of the LORD to
      Zerubbabel:
 'Not by might nor by power, but by
      My Spirit,'
 Says the LORD of hosts."

Zechariah 4:6

Those who wait on the LORD
Shall renew their strength;
They shall mount up with wings
      like eagles,
They shall run and not be weary,
They shall walk and not faint.

Isaiah 40:31

Faith 🕊

Now faith is the substance of things hoped for, the evidence of things not seen.

Hebrews 11:1

So then faith comes by hearing, and hearing by the word of God.

Romans 10:17

Jesus answered and said to them, "Have faith in God.

"For assuredly, I say to you, whoever says to this mountain, 'Be removed and be cast into the sea,' and does not doubt in his heart, but believes that those things he says will be done, he will have whatever he says.

"Therefore I say to you, whatever things you ask when you pray, believe that you receive them, and you will have them."

Mark 11:22–24

But without faith it is impossible to please Him, for he who comes to God must believe that He is, and that He is a rewarder of those who diligently seek Him.

Hebrews 11:6

Jesus said to him, "If you can believe, all things are possible to him who believes."

Mark 9:23

That the genuineness of your faith, being much more precious than gold that perishes, though it is tested by fire, may be found to praise, honor, and glory at the revelation of Jesus Christ, whom having not seen you love. Though now you do not see Him, yet believing, you rejoice with joy inexpressible and full of glory, receiving the end of your faith—the salvation of your souls.

1 Peter 1:7–9

Whatever is born of God overcomes the world. And this is the victory that has overcome the world—our faith.

1 John 5:4

A woman who had a flow of blood for twelve years came from behind and touched the hem of His garment.

For she said to herself, "If only I may touch His garment, I shall be made well."

But Jesus turned around, and when He saw her He said, "Be of good cheer, daughter; your faith has made you well." And the woman was made well from that hour.

Matthew 9:20–22

When He had come into the house, the blind men came to Him. And Jesus said to them, "Do you believe that I am able to do this?" They said to Him, "Yes, Lord."

Then He touched their eyes, saying, "According to your faith let it be to you."

Matthew 9:28, 29

Is anyone among you sick? Let him call for the elders of the church, and let them pray over him, anointing him with oil in the name of the Lord.

And the prayer of faith will save the sick, and the Lord will raise him up. And if he has committed sins, he will be forgiven.

James 5:14, 15

Love ✒

Though I speak with the tongues of men and of angels, but have not love, I have become sounding brass or a clanging cymbal.

And though I have the gift of prophecy, and understand all mysteries and all knowledge, and though I have all faith, so that I could remove mountains, but have not love, I am nothing.

And though I bestow all my goods to feed the poor, and though I give my body to be burned, but have not love, it profits me nothing.

Love suffers long and is kind; love does not envy; love does not parade itself, is not puffed up; does not behave rudely, does not seek its own, is not provoked, thinks no evil; does not rejoice in iniquity, but rejoices in the truth; bears all things, believes all things, hopes all things, endures all things.

Love never fails. But whether there are prophecies, they will fail; whether there are tongues, they will cease; whether there is knowledge, it will vanish away. And now abide faith, hope, love, these three; but the greatest of these is love.

1 Corinthians 13:1–8, 13

Beloved, let us love one another, for love is of God; and everyone who loves is born of God and knows God.

He who does not love does not know God, for God is love.

1 John 4:7, 8

In this is love, not that we loved God, but that He loved us and sent His Son to be the propitiation for our sins.

Beloved, if God so loved us, we also ought to love one another.

No one has seen God at any time. If we love one another, God abides in us, and His love has been perfected in us.

1 John 4:10–12

He who has My commandments and keeps them, it is he who loves Me. And he who loves Me will be loved by My Father, and I will love him and manifest Myself to him.

John 14:21

As the Father loved Me, I also have loved you; abide in My love.

If you keep My commandments, you will abide in My love, just as I have kept My Father's commandments and abide in His love.

John 15:9, 10

The LORD has appeared of old to me,
    saying:
"Yes, I have loved you with an everlasting
    love;
Therefore with lovingkindness I have
    drawn you."

Jeremiah 31:3

The Father Himself loves you, because you have loved Me, and have believed that I came forth from God.

John 16:27

God demonstrates His own love toward us, in that while we were still sinners, Christ died for us.

Romans 5:8

God so loved the world that He gave His only begotten Son, that whoever believes in Him should not perish but have everlasting life.

John 3:16

I am persuaded that neither death nor life, nor angels nor principalities nor powers, nor things present nor things to come, nor height nor depth, nor any other created thing, shall be able to separate us from the love of God which is in Christ Jesus our Lord.

Romans 8:38, 39

God has not given us a spirit of fear, but of power and of love and of a sound mind.

Who has saved us and called us with a holy calling, not according to our works, but according to His own purpose and grace which was given to us in Christ Jesus before time began.

2 Timothy 1:7, 9

I love those who love me,
And those who seek me diligently will
find me.

Proverbs 8:17

Promises About Your Personal Relationships

Single and Satisfied

> I will betroth you to Me forever;
> Yes, I will betroth you to Me
> In righteousness and justice,
> In lovingkindness and mercy;
>
> *Hosea 2:19*

> But I say to the unmarried and to the widows: It is good for them if they remain even as I am.
>
> *1 Corinthians 7:8*

> But as God has distributed to each one, as the Lord has called each one, so let him walk. And so I ordain in all the churches.
> Are you bound to a wife? Do not seek to be loosed. Are you loosed from a wife? Do not seek a wife.
> But even if you do marry, you have not sinned; and if a virgin marries, she has not sinned. Nevertheless such will have trouble in the flesh, but I would spare you.
>
> *1 Corinthians 7:17, 27, 28*

> Delight yourself also in the LORD, and He shall give you the desires of your heart.
>
> *Psalm 37:4*

But I want you to be without care. He who is unmarried cares for the things of the Lord—how he may please the Lord.

But he who is married cares about the things of the world—how he may please his wife.

And this I say for your own profit, not that I may put a leash on you, but for what is proper, and that you may serve the Lord without distraction.

1 Corinthians 7:32, 33, 35

Nevertheless he who stands steadfast in his heart, having no necessity, but has power over his own will, and has so determined in his heart that he will keep his virgin, does well.

1 Corinthians 7:37

Marriage is honorable among all, and the bed undefiled; but fornicators and adulterers God will judge.

Hebrews 13:4

Trust in the LORD with all your heart, and lean not on your own understanding; in all your ways acknowledge Him, and He shall direct your paths.

Proverbs 3:5, 6

Therefore, my brethren, you also have become dead to the law through the body of Christ, that you may be married to another—to Him who was raised from the dead, that we should bear fruit to God.

Romans 7:4

But let each one examine his own work, and then he will have rejoicing in himself alone, and not in another.

Galatians 6:4

To knowledge self-control, to self-control perseverance, to perseverance godliness, to godliness brotherly kindness, and to brotherly kindness love.

For if these things are yours and abound, you will be neither barren nor unfruitful in the knowledge of our Lord Jesus Christ.

2 Peter 1:6–8

Unsaved Family Members ✐

So they said, "Believe on the Lord Jesus Christ, and you will be saved, you and your household."

Acts 16:31

Who will tell you words by which you and all your household will be saved.

Acts 11:14

Even so it is not the will of your Father who is in heaven that one of these little ones should perish.

Matthew 18:14

I will pour water on him who is thirsty,
And floods on the dry ground;
I will pour My Spirit on your descendants,
And My blessing on your offspring.

Isaiah 44:3

The Lord is not slack concerning His promise, as some count slackness, but is longsuffering toward us, not willing that any should perish but that all should come to repentance.

2 Peter 3:9

Who among you fears the LORD?
Who obeys the voice of His Servant?
Who walks in darkness
And has no light?
Let him trust in the name of the LORD
And rely upon his God.

Isaiah 50:10

Cast your burden on the LORD, and He shall sustain you; He shall never permit the righteous to be moved.

Psalm 55:22

Keep justice, and do righteousness, for My salvation is about to come, and My righteousness to be revealed.

Isaiah 56:1

Nevertheless I tell you the truth. It is to your advantage that I go away; for if I do not go away, the Helper will not come to you; but if I depart, I will send Him to you.

And when He has come, He will convict the world of sin, and of righteousness, and of judgment.

John 16:7, 8

Train up a child in the way he should go, and when he is old he will not depart from it.

Proverbs 22:6

Forgiving Others ✒

If you forgive men their trespasses, your heavenly Father will also forgive you.

But if you do not forgive men their trespasses, neither will your Father forgive your trespasses.

Matthew 6:14,15

Then Peter came to Him and said, "Lord, how often shall my brother sin against me, and I forgive him? Up to seven times?"

Jesus said to him, "I do not say to you, up to seven times, but up to seventy times seven."

Matthew 18:21, 22

Take heed to yourselves. If your brother sins against you, rebuke him; and if he repents, forgive him.

Luke 17:3

Whenever you stand praying, if you have anything against anyone, forgive him, that your Father in heaven may also forgive you your trespasses.

Mark 11:25

Bearing with one another, and forgiving one another, if anyone has a complaint against another; even as Christ forgave you, so you also must do.

Colossians 3:13

Brethren, I do not count myself to have apprehended; but one thing I do, forgetting those things which are behind and reaching forward to those things which are ahead, I press toward the goal for the prize of the upward call of God in Christ Jesus.

Philippians 3:13, 14

Do not remember the former things,
Nor consider the things of old.
Behold, I will do a new thing,
Now it shall spring forth;
Shall you not know it?
I will even make a road in the wilderness
And rivers in the desert.

Isaiah 43:18, 19

For we know Him who said, "Vengeance is Mine, I will repay," says the Lord. And again, "The LORD will judge His people."

Hebrews 10:30

Blessed are those who are persecuted for righteousness' sake, for theirs is the kingdom of heaven.

Blessed are you when they revile and persecute you, and say all kinds of evil against you falsely for My sake.

Rejoice and be exceedingly glad, for great is your reward in heaven, for so they persecuted the prophets who were before you.

Matthew 5:10–12

Now thanks be to God who always leads us in triumph in Christ, and through us diffuses the fragrance of His knowledge in every place.

2 Corinthians 2:14

Christian Friendships ✒

That which we have seen and heard we declare to you, that you also may have fellowship with us; and truly our fellowship is with the Father and with His Son Jesus Christ.

But if we walk in the light as He is in the light, we have fellowship with one another, and the blood of Jesus Christ His Son cleanses us from all sin.

1 John 1:3, 7

Walk in love, as Christ also has loved us and given Himself for us, an offering and a sacrifice to God for a sweet-smelling aroma.

Speaking to one another in psalms and hymns and spiritual songs, singing and making melody in your heart to the Lord, for we are members of His body, of His flesh and of His bones.

Ephesians 5:2,19, 30

Let the word of Christ dwell in you richly in all wisdom, teaching and admonishing one another in psalms and hymns and spiritual songs, singing with grace in your hearts to the Lord.

Colossians 3:16

That their hearts may be encouraged, being knit together in love, and attaining to all riches of the full assurance of understanding, to the knowledge of the mystery of God, both of the Father and of Christ.

Colossians 2:2

Then those who feared the LORD spoke to
     one another,
And the LORD listened and heard them;
So a book of remembrance was written
     before Him
For those who fear the LORD
And who meditate on His name.

Malachi 3:16

Now behold, two of them were traveling that same day to a village called Emmaus, which was seven miles from Jerusalem.

And they talked together of all these things which had happened.

So it was, while they conversed and reasoned, that Jesus Himself drew near and went with them.

Luke 24:13–15

We took sweet counsel together, and walked to the house of God in the throng.

Psalm 55:14

Now may the God of patience and comfort grant you to be like-minded toward one another, according to Christ Jesus, that you may with one mind and one mouth glorify the God and Father of our Lord Jesus Christ.

Therefore receive one another, just as Christ also received us, to the glory of God.

Romans 15:5–7

Now I plead with you, brethren, by the name of our Lord Jesus Christ, that you all speak the same thing, and that there be no divisions among you, but that you be perfectly joined together in the same mind and in the same judgment.

1 Corinthians 1:10

Bear one another's burdens, and so fulfill the law of Christ.

Therefore, as we have opportunity, let us do good to all, especially to those who are of the household of faith.

Galatians 6:2, 10

Promises When
You Feel . . .

Dissatisfied 🕊

The young lions lack and suffer hunger; but those who seek the LORD shall not lack any good thing.

Psalm 34:10

I will pour water on him who is thirsty,
And floods on the dry ground;
I will pour My Spirit on your descendants,
And My blessing on your offspring.

Isaiah 44:3

Trust in the LORD, and do good; dwell in the land, and feed on His faithfulness.

Psalm 37:3

I know how to be abased, and I know how to abound. Everywhere and in all things I have learned both to be full and to be hungry, both to abound and to suffer need.

I can do all things through Christ who strengthens me.

Philippians 4:12, 13

A man will be satisifed with good by the fruit of his mouth, and the recompense of a man's hands will be rendered to him.

Proverbs 12:14

O God, You are my God;
Early will I seek You;
My soul thirsts for You;
My flesh longs for You. . . .
So I have looked for You in the sanctuary,
To see Your power and Your glory.
Because Your lovingkindness is better
      than life,
My lips shall praise You.
Thus I will bless You while I live;
I will lift up my hands in Your name.
My soul shall be satisfied as with marrow
      and fatness,
And my mouth shall praise You with
      joyful lips.

Psalm 63:1–5

Blessed are those who hunger and thirst for righteousness, for they shall be filled.

Matthew 5:6

Ho! Everyone who thirsts,
Come to the waters;
And you who have no money,
Come, buy and eat.
Yes, come, buy wine and milk
Without money and without price.

Isaiah 55:1

God is able to make all grace abound toward you, that you, always having all sufficiency in all things, may have an abundance for every good work.

2 Corinthians 9:8

Bless the LORD, O my soul,
And forget not all His benefits:
Who forgives all your iniquities,
Who heals all your diseases,
Who redeems your life from destruction,
Who crowns you with lovingkindness and
	tender mercies,
Who satisfies your mouth with
	good things,
So that your youth is renewed like
	the eagle's.

Psalm 103:2–5

He satisfies the longing soul, and fills the hungry soul with goodness.

Psalm 107:9

Confused ✒

God is not the author of confusion but of peace, as in all the churches of the saints.

1 Corinthians 14:33

For God has not given us a spirit of fear, but of power and of love and of a sound mind.

2 Timothy 1:7

For where envy and self-seeking exist, confusion and every evil thing are there.

But the wisdom that is from above is first pure, then peaceable, gentle, willing to yield, full of mercy and good fruits, without partiality and without hypocrisy.

Now the fruit of righteousness is sown in peace by those who make peace.

James 3:16–18

The Lord GOD will help Me; therefore I will not be disgraced; therefore I have set My face like a flint, and I know that I will not be ashamed.

Isaiah 50:7

If any of you lacks wisdom, let him ask of God, who gives to all liberally and without reproach, and it will be given to him.

James 1:5

Trust in the LORD with all your heart,
And lean not on your own understanding;
In all your ways acknowledge Him,
And He shall direct your paths.

Proverbs 3:5, 6

I will instruct you and teach you in the way you should go; I will guide you with My eye.

Psalm 32:8

Great peace have those who love Your law, and nothing causes them to stumble.

Psalm 119:165

Cast your burden on the LORD, and He shall sustain you; He shall never permit the righteous to be moved.

Psalm 55:22

Discouraged ✈

So the ransomed of the LORD shall return,
And come to Zion with singing,
With everlasting joy on their heads.
They shall obtain joy and gladness;
Sorrow and sighing shall flee away.

Isaiah 51:11

In this you greatly rejoice, though now for a little while, if need be, you have been grieved by various trials, that the genuineness of your faith, being much more precious than gold that perishes, though it is tested by fire, may be found to praise, honor, and glory at the revelation of Jesus Christ, whom having not seen you love.

Though now you do not see Him, yet believing, you rejoice with joy inexpressible and full of glory, receiving the end of your faith—the salvation of your souls.

1 Peter 1:6–9

Let not your heart be troubled; you believe in God, believe also in Me.

John 14:1

Be anxious for nothing, but in everything by prayer and supplication, with thanksgiving, let your requests be made known to God; and the peace of God, which surpasses all understanding, will guard your hearts and minds through Christ Jesus.

Philippians 4:6–7

Though I walk in the midst of trouble, You
    will revive me;
You will stretch out Your hand
Against the wrath of my enemies,
And Your right hand will save me.

Psalm 138:7

The LORD is my light and my salvation;
Whom shall I fear?
The LORD is the strength of my life;
Of whom shall I be afraid?
When the wicked came against me
To eat up my flesh,
My enemies and foes,
They stumbled and fell.
Though an army may encamp against me,
My heart shall not fear;
Though war should rise against me,
In this I will be confident.

Psalm 27:1–3

Lonely ✸

Let your conduct be without covetousness; be content with such things as you have. For He Himself has said, "I will never leave you nor forsake you."

Hebrews 13:5

Teaching them to observe all things that I have commanded you; and lo, I am with you always, even to the end of the age. Amen.

Matthew 28:20

The LORD will not forsake His people, for His great name's sake, because it has pleased the LORD to make you His people.

1 Samuel 12:22

Fear not, for I am with you;
Be not dismayed, for I am your God.
I will strengthen you,
Yes, I will help you,
I will uphold you with My righteous
        right hand.

Isaiah 41:10

I will not leave you orphans; I will come to you.

John 14:18

Let not your heart be troubled; you believe in God, believe also in Me.

John 14:1

The eternal God is your refuge,
And underneath are the everlasting arms;
He will thrust out the enemy from
     before you,
And will say, "Destroy!"

Deuteronomy 33:27

He heals the brokenhearted and binds up their wounds.

Psalm 147:3

(For the LORD your God is a merciful God), He will not forsake you nor destroy you, nor forget the covenant of your fathers which He swore to them.

Deuteronomy 4:31

Be strong and of good courage, do not fear nor be afraid of them; for the LORD your God, He is the One who goes with you. He will not leave you nor forsake you.

Deuteronomy 31:6

When my father and my mother forsake me, then the LORD will take care of me.

Psalm 27:10

"For the mountains shall depart
  And the hills be removed,
  But My kindness shall not depart
    from you,
  Nor shall My covenant of peace be
    removed,"
Says the LORD, who has mercy on you.

Isaiah 54:10

Casting all your care upon Him, for He cares for you.

1 Peter 5:7

God is our refuge and strength, a very present help in trouble.

Psalm 46:1

Let not your heart be troubled; you believe in God, believe also in Me.

John 14:1

He heals the brokenhearted and binds up their wounds.

Psalm 147:3

Depressed ✒

The righteous cry out, and the LORD hears, and delivers them out of all their troubles.

Psalm 34:17

For His anger is but for a moment,
His favor is for life;
Weeping may endure for a night,
But joy comes in the morning.

Psalm 30:5

Beloved, do not think it strange concerning the fiery trial which is to try you, as though some strange thing happened to you; but rejoice to the extent that you partake of Christ's sufferings, that when His glory is revealed, you may also be glad with exceeding joy.

1 Peter 4:12, 13

Fear not, for I am with you;
Be not dismayed, for I am your God.
I will strengthen you,
Yes, I will help you,
I will uphold you with My righteous
    right hand.

Isaiah 41:10

To console those who mourn in Zion,
To give them beauty for ashes,
The oil of joy for mourning,
The garment of praise for the spirit
    of heaviness;
That they may be called trees of
    righteousness,
The planting of the LORD, that He may
    be glorified.

Isaiah 61:3

Blessed be the God and Father of our Lord Jesus Christ, the Father of mercies and God of all comfort, who comforts us in all our tribulation, that we may be able to comfort those who are in any trouble, with the comfort with which we ourselves are comforted by God.

2 Corinthians 1:3, 4

Finally, brethren, whatever things are true, whatever things are noble, whatever things are just, whatever things are pure, whatever things are lovely, whatever things are of good report, if there is any virtue and if there is anything praiseworthy—meditate on these things.

Philippians 4:8

He heals the brokenhearted and binds up their wounds.

Psalm 147:3

Angry ✒

So then, my beloved brethren, let every man be swift to hear, slow to speak, slow to wrath; for the wrath of man does not produce the righteousness of God.

James 1:19, 20

"Be angry, and do not sin": do not let the sun go down on your wrath.

Ephesians 4:26

A soft answer turns away wrath, but a harsh word stirs up anger.

Proverbs 15:1

If you forgive men their trespasses, your heavenly Father will also forgive you.

Matthew 6:14

He who is slow to wrath has great understanding, but he who is impulsive exalts folly.

Proverbs 14:29

He who is slow to anger is better than the mighty, and he who rules his spirit than he who takes a city.

Proverbs 16:32

Do not hasten in your spirit to be angry, for anger rests in the bosom of fools.

Ecclesiastes 7:9

Beloved, do not avenge yourselves, but rather give place to wrath; for it is written, "Vengeance is Mine, I will repay," says the Lord.

Romans 12:19

If your enemy is hungry, give him bread
    to eat;
And if he is thirsty, give him water
    to drink;
For so you will heap coals of fire on
    his head,
And the LORD will reward you.

Proverbs 25:21, 22

For we know Him who said, "Vengeance is Mine, I will repay," says the Lord. And again, "The LORD will judge His people."

Hebrews 10:30

Let all bitterness, wrath, anger, clamor, and evil speaking be put away from you, with all malice.

And be kind to one another, tenderhearted, forgiving one another, just as God in Christ forgave you.

Ephesians 4:31, 32

But I say to you that whoever is angry with his brother without a cause shall be in danger of the judgment. And whoever says to his brother, "Raca!" shall be in danger of the council. But whoever says, "You fool!" shall be in danger of hell fire.

Therefore if you bring your gift to the altar, and there remember that your brother has something against you, leave your gift there before the altar, and go your way. First be reconciled to your brother, and then come and offer your gift.

Matthew 5:22–24

A wise man fears and departs from evil,
But a fool rages and is self-confident.
A quick-tempered man acts foolishly,
And a man of wicked intentions is hated.

Proverbs 14:16, 17

Now you yourselves are to put off all these: anger, wrath, malice, blasphemy, filthy language out of your mouth.

Colossians 3:8

Cease from anger, and forsake wrath; do not fret—it only causes harm.

Psalm 37:8

Worried ✈

Casting all your care upon Him, for He cares for you.

1 Peter 5:7

Be anxious for nothing, but in everything by prayer and supplication, with thanksgiving, let your requests be made known to God; and the peace of God, which surpasses all understanding, will guard your hearts and minds through Christ Jesus.

Philippians 4:6, 7

Let the peace of God rule in your hearts, to which also you were called in one body; and be thankful.

Colossians 3:15

You will keep him in perfect peace, whose mind is stayed on You, because he trusts in You.

Isaiah 26:3

To be carnally minded is death, but to be spiritually minded is life and peace.

Romans 8:6

Therefore I say to you, do not worry about your life, what you will eat or what you will drink; nor about your body, what you will put on. Is not life more than food and the body more than clothing?

Look at the birds of the air, for they neither sow nor reap nor gather into barns; yet your heavenly Father feeds them. Are you not of more value than they?

Which of you by worrying can add one cubit to his stature?

So why do you worry about clothing? Consider the lilies of the field, how they grow: they neither toil nor spin; and yet I say to you that even Solomon in all his glory was not arrayed like one of these.

Now if God so clothes the grass of the field, which today is, and tomorrow is thrown into the oven, will He not much more clothe you, O you of little faith? Therefore do not worry, saying, "What shall we eat?" or "What shall we drink?" or "What shall we wear?"

For after all these things the Gentiles seek. For your heavenly Father knows that you need all these things.

Matthew 6:25–32

I will both lie down in peace, and sleep; for You alone, O LORD, make me dwell in safety.

Psalm 4:8

My God shall supply all your need according to His riches in glory by Christ Jesus.

Philippians 4:19

When you lie down, you will not be afraid; yes, you will lie down and your sleep will be sweet.

Proverbs 3:24

For we who have believed do enter that rest, as He has said: "So I swore in My wrath, 'They shall not enter My rest,' although the works were finished from the foundation of the world."

There remains therefore a rest for the people of God.

Hebrews 4:3, 9

Tempted ✈

Let him who thinks he stands take heed lest he fall.

No temptation has overtaken you except such as is common to man; but God is faithful, who will not allow you to be tempted beyond what you are able, but with the temptation will also make the way of escape, that you may be able to bear it.

1 Corinthians 10:12, 13

Seeing then that we have a great High Priest who has passed through the heavens, Jesus the Son of God, let us hold fast our confession.

For we do not have a High Priest who cannot sympathize with our weaknesses, but was in all points tempted as we are, yet without sin. Let us therefore come boldly to the throne of grace, that we may obtain mercy and find grace to help in time of need.

Hebrews 4:14–16

In that He Himself has suffered, being tempted, He is able to aid those who are tempted.

Hebrews 2:18

The Lord knows how to deliver the godly out of temptations and to reserve the unjust under punishment for the day of judgment.

2 Peter 2:9

Sin shall not have dominion over you, for you are not under law but under grace.

Romans 6:14

Your word I have hidden in my heart, that I might not sin against You!

Psalm 119:11

Let no one say when he is tempted, "I am tempted by God"; for God cannot be tempted by evil, nor does He Himself tempt anyone.

But each one is tempted when he is drawn away by his own desires and enticed.

James 1:13, 14

Be sober, be vigilant; because your adversary the devil walks about like a roaring lion, seeking whom he may devour.

Resist him, steadfast in the faith, knowing that the same sufferings are experienced by your brotherhood in the world.

1 Peter 5:8, 9

Finally, my brethren, be strong in the Lord and in the power of His might.

Put on the whole armor of God, that you may be able to stand against the wiles of the devil.

Above all, [take] the shield of faith with which you will be able to quench all the fiery darts of the wicked one.

Ephesians 6:10, 11, 16

Submit to God. Resist the devil and he will flee from you.

James 4:7

You are of God, little children, and have overcome them, because He who is in you is greater than he who is in the world.

1 John 4:4

Blessed is the man who endures temptation; for when he has been approved, he will receive the crown of life which the Lord has promised to those who love Him.

James 1:12

Promises When You Are . . .

Worried by Finances 🕊

I pray that you may prosper in all things and be in health, just as your soul prospers.

3 John 2

The young lions lack and suffer hunger; but those who seek the LORD shall not lack any good thing.

Psalm 34:10

I have been young, and now am old; yet I have not seen the righteous forsaken, nor his descendants begging bread.

Psalm 37:25

Do not worry, saying, "What shall we eat?" or "What shall we drink?" or "What shall we wear?"'

For after all these things the Gentiles seek. For your heavenly Father knows that you need all these things.

But seek first the kingdom of God and His righteousness, and all these things shall be added to you.

Matthew 6:31–33

The LORD is my shepherd; I shall not want.

Psalm 23:1

The LORD will grant you plenty of goods, in the fruit of your body, in the increase of your livestock, and in the produce of your ground, in the land of which the LORD swore to your fathers to give you.

The LORD will open to you His good treasure, the heavens, to give the rain to your land in its season, and to bless all the work of your hand. You shall lend to many nations, but you shall not borrow.

And the LORD will make you the head and not the tail; you shall be above only, and not be beneath, if you heed the commandments of the LORD your God, which I command you today, and are careful to observe them.

Deuteronomy 28:11–13

My God shall supply all your need according to His riches in glory by Christ Jesus.

Philippians 4:19

Heal the sick, cleanse the lepers, raise the dead, cast out demons. Freely you have received, freely give.

Matthew 10:8

I have taught you in the way of wisdom; I have led you in right paths.

Proverbs 4:11

Give, and it will be given to you: good measure, pressed down, shaken together, and running over will be put into your bosom. For with the same measure that you use, it will be measured back to you.

Luke 6:38

On the first day of the week let each one of you lay something aside, storing up as he may prosper, that there be no collections when I come.

1 Corinthians 16:2

But this I say: He who sows sparingly will also reap sparingly, and he who sows bountifully will also reap bountifully.

So let each one give as he purposes in his heart, not grudgingly or of necessity; for God loves a cheerful giver.

And God is able to make all grace abound toward you, that you, always having all sufficiency in all things, may have an abundance for every good work.

2 Corinthians 9:6–8

Bewildered by God 🕊

"For My thoughts are not your thoughts,
  Nor are your ways My ways," says
    the Lord.
"For as the heavens are higher than
    the earth,
  So are My ways higher than your ways,
  And My thoughts than your thoughts."
                              Isaiah 55:8, 9

Call to Me, and I will answer you, and show you great and mighty things, which you do not know.
                              Jeremiah 33:3

What then shall we say to these things? If God is for us, who can be against us?
                              Romans 8:31

Who shall separate us from the love of Christ? Shall tribulation, or distress, or persecution, or famine, or nakedness, or peril, or sword?
   As it is written: "For Your sake we are killed all day long; we are accounted as sheep for the slaughter."
   Yet in all these things we are more than conquerors through Him who loved us.
                              Romans 8:35–37

No temptation has overtaken you except such as is common to man; but God is faithful, who will not allow you to be tempted beyond what you are able, but with the temptation will also make the way of escape, that you may be able to bear it.

1 Corinthians 10:13

Many are the afflictions of the righteous, but the LORD delivers him out of them all.

Psalm 34:19

Cast your burden on the LORD, and He shall sustain you; He shall never permit the righteous to be moved.

Psalm 55:22

Fear not, for I am with you;
Be not dismayed, for I am your God.
I will strengthen you,
Yes, I will help you,
I will uphold you with My righteous
right hand.

Isaiah 41:10

We know that all things work together for good to those who love God, to those who are the called according to His purpose.

Romans 8:28

As for God, His way is perfect; the word of the LORD is proven; He is a shield to all who trust in Him.

Psalm 18:30

The LORD will perfect that which concerns me; Your mercy, O LORD, endures forever; do not forsake the works of Your hands.

Psalm 138:8

Let us hold fast the confession of our hope without wavering, for He who promised is faithful.

Hebrews 10:23

I will make an everlasting covenant with them, that I will not turn away from doing them good; but I will put My fear in their hearts so that they will not depart from Me.

Jeremiah 32:40

Disillusioned by Life ✒

The LORD is good, a stronghold in the day of trouble; and He knows those who trust in Him.

Nahum 1:7

We are hard pressed on every side, yet not crushed; we are perplexed, but not in despair; persecuted, but not forsaken; struck down, but not destroyed.

2 Corinthians 4:8, 9

Though I walk in the midst of trouble,
    You will revive me;
You will stretch out Your hand
Against the wrath of my enemies,
And Your right hand will save me.

Psalm 138:7

Therefore do not worry about tomorrow, for tomorrow will worry about its own things. Sufficient for the day is its own trouble.

Matthew 6:34

Let not your heart be troubled; you believe in God, believe also in Me.

John 14:1

We know that all things work together for good to those who love God, to those who are the called according to His purpose.

Romans 8:28

I will be glad and rejoice in Your mercy, for You have considered my trouble; You have known my soul in adversities.

Psalm 31:7

I will lift up my eyes to the hills—
From whence comes my help?
My help comes from the LORD,
Who made heaven and earth.

Psalm 121:1, 2

For we do not have a High Priest who cannot sympathize with our weaknesses, but was in all points tempted as we are, yet without sin. Let us therefore come boldly to the throne of grace, that we may obtain mercy and find grace to help in time of need.

Hebrews 4:15, 16

Casting all your care upon Him, for He cares for you.

1 Peter 5:7

Do not worry about tomorrow, for tomorrow will worry about its own things. Sufficient for the day is its own trouble.

Matthew 6:34

Blessed be the God and Father of our Lord Jesus Christ, the Father of mercies and God of all comfort, who comforts us in all our tribulation, that we may be able to comfort those who are in any trouble, with the comfort with which we ourselves are comforted by God.

2 Corinthians 1:3, 4

Be anxious for nothing, but in everything by prayer and supplication, with thanksgiving, let your requests be made known to God; and the peace of God, which surpasses all understanding, will guard your hearts and minds through Christ Jesus.

Philippians 4:6, 7

Sick and in Pain

Is anyone among you sick? Let him call for the elders of the church, and let them pray over him, anointing him with oil in the name of the Lord.

And the prayer of faith will save the sick, and the Lord will raise him up. And if he has committed sins, he will be forgiven.

James 5:14–15

You will keep him in perfect peace,
Whose mind is stayed on You,
Because he trusts in You.
Trust in the LORD forever,
For in YAH, the LORD, is everlasting
    strength.

Isaiah 26:3–4

Heal me, O LORD, and I shall be healed; save me, and I shall be saved, for You are my praise.

Jeremiah 17:14

Who Himself bore our sins in His own body on the tree, that we, having died to sins, might live for righteousness—by whose stripes you were healed.

1 Peter 2:24

For all things are for your sakes, that grace, having spread through the many, may cause thanksgiving to abound to the glory of God.

Therefore we do not lose heart. Even though our outward man is perishing, yet the inward man is being renewed day by day.

For our light affliction, which is but for a moment, is working for us a far more exceeding and eternal weight of glory, while we do not look at the things which are seen, but at the things which are not seen. For the things which are seen are temporary, but the things which are not seen are eternal.

2 Corinthians 4:15–18

And I said, "This is my anguish;
But I will remember the years of the right
    hand of the Most High."
I will remember the works of the LORD;
Surely I will remember Your wonders
    of old.
I will also meditate on all Your work,
And talk of Your deeds.
Your way, O God, is in the sanctuary;
Who is so great a God as our God?
You are the God who does wonders;
You have declared Your strength among
    the peoples.

Psalm 77:10–14

Yea, though I walk through the valley of the shadow of death, I will fear no evil; for You are with me; Your rod and Your staff, they comfort me.

Psalm 23:4

For we know that if our earthly house, this tent, is destroyed, we have a building from God, a house not made with hands, eternal in the heavens.

2 Corinthians 5:1

For this is God, our God forever and ever; He will be our guide even to death.

Psalm 48:14

But God will redeem my soul from the power of the grave, for He shall receive me.

Psalm 49:15

I call to remembrance my song in the night; I meditate within my heart, and my spirit makes diligent search.

Psalm 77:6

Stressed Out ✒

Peace I leave with you, My peace I give to you; not as the world gives do I give to you. Let not your heart be troubled, neither let it be afraid.

John 14:27

Be anxious for nothing, but in everything by prayer and supplication, with thanksgiving, let your requests be made known to God; and the peace of God, which surpasses all understanding, will guard your hearts and minds through Christ Jesus.

Finally, brethren, whatever things are true, whatever things are noble, whatever things are just, whatever things are pure, whatever things are lovely, whatever things are of good report, if there is any virtue and if there is anything praise-worthy—meditate on these things.

Philippians 4:6–8

Fear not, for I am with you;
Be not dismayed, for I am your God.
I will strengthen you,
Yes, I will help you,
I will uphold you with My righteous
    right hand.

Isaiah 41:10

He makes me to lie down in green
 pastures;
He leads me beside the still waters.
He restores my soul;
He leads me in the paths of righteousness
For His name's sake.
Yea, though I walk through the valley of
 the shadow of death,
I will fear no evil;
For You are with me;
Your rod and Your staff, they comfort me.

Psalm 23:2–4

Casting all your care upon Him, for He cares for you.

Be sober, be vigilant; because your adversary the devil walks about like a roaring lion, seeking whom he may devour.

Resist him, steadfast in the faith, knowing that the same sufferings are experienced by your brotherhood in the world.

But may the God of all grace, who called us to His eternal glory by Christ Jesus, after you have suffered a while, perfect, establish, strengthen, and settle you.

1 Peter 5:7–10

God is our refuge and strength,
A very present help in trouble.
Therefore we will not fear,
Even though the earth be removed,
And though the mountains be carried into
    the midst of the sea;
Though its waters roar and be troubled,
Though the mountains shake with its
    swelling. Selah

Psalm 46:1–3

"Be angry, and do not sin": do not let the sun go down on your wrath, nor give place to the devil.

Ephesians 4:26–27

But He was in the stern, asleep on a pillow. And they awoke Him and said to Him, "Teacher, do You not care that we are perishing?"

Then He arose and rebuked the wind, and said to the sea, "Peace, be still!" And the wind ceased and there was a great calm.

But He said to them, "Why are you so fearful? How is it that you have no faith?"

Mark 4:38–40

Surely He shall deliver you from the snare
    of the fowler
And from the perilous pestilence.
He shall cover you with His feathers,
And under His wings you shall take refuge;
His truth shall be your shield and buckler.
You shall not be afraid of the terror
    by night,
Nor of the arrow that flies by day,
Nor of the pestilence that walks
    in darkness,
Nor of the destruction that lays waste
    at noonday.
A thousand may fall at your side,
And ten thousand at your right hand;
But it shall not come near you.

Psalm 91:3–7

Whenever I am afraid,
I will trust in You.
In God (I will praise His word),
In God I have put my trust;
I will not fear.
What can flesh do to me?

Psalm 56:3–4

Discontent ✒

"Therefore do not worry, saying, 'What shall we eat?' or 'What shall we drink?' or 'What shall we wear?'

"For after all these things the Gentiles seek. For your heavenly Father knows that you need all these things.

"But seek first the kingdom of God and His righteousness, and all these things shall be added to you.

"Therefore do not worry about tomorrow, for tomorrow will worry about its own things. Sufficient for the day is its own trouble."

Matthew 6:31–34

You will keep him in perfect peace,
Whose mind is stayed on You,
Because he trusts in You.
Trust in the LORD forever,
For in YAH, the LORD, is everlasting
    strength.

Isaiah 26:3–4

Let your conduct be without covetousness; be content with such things as you have. For He Himself has said, "I will never leave you nor forsake you."

So we may boldly say: "The LORD is my helper; I will not fear. What can man do to me?"

Hebrews 13:5–6

Be anxious for nothing, but in everything by prayer and supplication, with thanksgiving, let your requests be made known to God; and the peace of God, which surpasses all understanding, will guard your hearts and minds through Christ Jesus.

Not that I speak in regard to need, for I have learned in whatever state I am, to be content: I know how to be abased, and I know how to abound. Everywhere and in all things I have learned both to be full and to be hungry, both to abound and to suffer need.

I can do all things through Christ who strengthens me.

Philippians 4:6, 7, 11–13

We know that all things work together for good to those who love God, to those who are the called according to His purpose.

Romans 8:28

Now godliness with contentment is great gain.

For we brought nothing into this world, and it is certain we can carry nothing out.

And having food and clothing, with these we shall be content.

1 Timothy 6:6–8

He who dwells in the secret place of the
    Most High
Shall abide under the shadow of
    the Almighty.
I will say of the LORD, "He is my refuge
    and my fortress;
My God, in Him I will trust."

Psalm 91:1–2

But I discipline my body and bring it into subjection, lest, when I have preached to others, I myself should become disqualified.

1 Corinthians 9:27

The LORD upholds all who fall,
And raises up all who are bowed down.
The eyes of all look expectantly to You,
And You give them their food in
    due season.
You open Your hand
And satisfy the desire of every living thing.

Psalm 145:14–16

To be carnally minded is death, but to be spiritually minded is life and peace.

Romans 8:6

Promises that
Jesus Is Your . . .

Companion 🕊

A man who has friends must himself be friendly, but there is a friend who sticks closer than a brother.

Proverbs 18:24

Let your conduct be without covetousness; be content with such things as you have. For He Himself has said, "I will never leave you nor forsake you."

Hebrews 13:5

No longer do I call you servants, for a servant does not know what his master is doing; but I have called you friends, for all things that I heard from My Father I have made known to you.

You did not choose Me, but I chose you and appointed you that you should go and bear fruit, and that your fruit should remain, that whatever you ask the Father in My name He may give you.

John 15:15, 16

Draw near to God and He will draw near to you. Cleanse your hands, you sinners; and purify your hearts, you double-minded.

James 4:8

"For the mountains shall depart
  And the hills be removed,
  But My kindness shall not depart
    from you,
  Nor shall My covenant of peace
    be removed,"
  Says the LORD, who has mercy on you.

Isaiah 54:10

Draw near to God and He will draw near to you. Cleanse your hands, you sinners; and purify your hearts, you double-minded.

James 4:8

When my father and my mother forsake me, then the LORD will take care of me.

Psalm 27:10

You are My friends if you do whatever I command you.

John 15:14

I will not leave you orphans; I will come to you.

John 14:18

Savior 🕊

Not by works of righteousness which we have done, but according to His mercy He saved us, through the washing of regeneration and renewing of the Holy Spirit, whom He poured out on us abundantly through Jesus Christ our Savior.

Titus 3:5, 6

We have seen and testify that the Father has sent the Son as Savior of the world.

1 John 4:14

My spirit has rejoiced in God my Savior.

Luke 1:47

We ourselves have heard Him and we know that this is indeed the Christ, the Savior of the world.

John 4:42b

The Son of Man has come to seek and to save that which was lost.

Luke 19:10

For God so loved the world that He gave His only begotten Son, that whoever believes in Him should not perish but have everlasting life.

John 3:16

Being justified freely by His grace through the redemption that is in Christ Jesus, whom God set forth as a propitiation by His blood, through faith, to demonstrate His righteousness, because in His forbearance God had passed over the sins that were previously committed.

Romans 3:24, 25

But God, who is rich in mercy, because of His great love with which He loved us, even when we were dead in trespasses, made us alive together with Christ (by grace you have been saved).

Ephesians 2:4, 5

Most assuredly, I say to you, he who believes in Me has everlasting life.

John 6:47

For by grace you have been saved through faith, and that not of yourselves; it is the gift of God, not of works, lest anyone should boast.

Ephesians 2:8, 9

If you confess with your mouth the Lord Jesus and believe in your heart that God has raised Him from the dead, you will be saved.

Romans 10:9

If anyone is in Christ, he is a new creation; old things have passed away; behold, all things have become new.

2 Corinthians 5:17

Who has saved us and called us with a holy calling, not according to our works, but according to His own purpose and grace which was given to us in Christ Jesus before time began.

2 Timothy 1:9

Nevertheless He saved them for His name's sake, that He might make His mighty power known.

Psalm 106:8

Deliverer ✐

The Spirit of the Lord GOD is upon Me,
Because the LORD has anointed Me
To preach good tidings to the poor;
He has sent Me to heal the brokenhearted,
To proclaim liberty to the captives,
And the opening of the prison to those
     who are bound.

Isaiah 61:1

You shall know the truth, and the truth shall make you free.

Therefore if the Son makes you free, you shall be free indeed.

John 8:32, 36

The law of the Spirit of life in Christ Jesus has made me free from the law of sin and death.

Romans 8:2

The Lord is the Spirit; and where the Spirit of the Lord is, there is liberty.

2 Corinthians 3:17

Having been set free from sin, and having become slaves of God, you have your fruit to holiness, and the end, everlasting life.

Romans 6:22

You have broken the yoke of his burden and the staff of his shoulder, the rod of his oppressor, as in the day of Midian.

Isaiah 9:4

I will be glad and rejoice in Your mercy,
For You have considered my trouble;
You have known my soul in adversities.

Psalm 31:7

Behold, I give you the authority to trample on serpents and scorpions, and over all the power of the enemy, and nothing shall by any means hurt you.

Luke 10:19

These signs will follow those who believe: In My name they will cast out demons; they will speak with new tongues.

Mark 16:17

They overcame him by the blood of the Lamb and by the word of their testimony, and they did not love their lives to the death.

Revelation 12:11

Example ✒

To this you were called, because Christ also suffered for us, leaving us an example, that you should follow His steps.

1 Peter 2:21

He who says he abides in Him ought himself also to walk just as He walked.

1 John 2:6

If I then, your Lord and Teacher, have washed your feet, you also ought to wash one another's feet.

For I have given you an example, that you should do as I have done to you.

John 13:14, 15

Let this mind be in you which was also in Christ Jesus, who, being in the form of God, did not consider it robbery to be equal with God, but made Himself of no reputation, taking the form of a bondservant, and coming in the likeness of men.

And being found in appearance as a man, He humbled Himself and became obedient to the point of death, even the death of the cross.

Philippians 2:5–8

Whoever desires to become great among you shall be your servant.

And whoever of you desires to be first shall be slave of all.

For even the Son of Man did not come to be served, but to serve, and to give His life a ransom for many.

Mark 10:43–45

A new commandment I give to you, that you love one another; as I have loved you, that you also love one another.

John 13:34

By this we know love, because He laid down His life for us. And we also ought to lay down our lives for the brethren.

1 John 3:16

Now may the God of patience and comfort grant you to be like-minded toward one another, according to Christ Jesus, that you may with one mind and one mouth glorify the God and Father of our Lord Jesus Christ.

Therefore receive one another, just as Christ also received us, to the glory of God.

Romans 15:5–7

Looking unto Jesus, the author and finisher of our faith, who for the joy that was set before Him endured the cross, despising the shame, and has sat down at the right hand of the throne of God.

For consider Him who endured such hostility from sinners against Himself, lest you become weary and discouraged in your souls.

Hebrews 12:2, 3

You know that He was manifested to take away our sins, and in Him there is no sin. Whoever abides in Him does not sin. Whoever sins has neither seen Him nor known Him. Little children, let no one deceive you. He who practices righteousness is righteous, just as He is righteous.

1 John 3:5–7

Guardian ✈

When you pass through the waters, I will be with you; and through the rivers, they shall not overflow you. When you walk through the fire, you shall not be burned, nor shall the flame scorch you.

Isaiah 43:2

But You, O LORD, are a shield for me, my glory and the One who lifts up my head.

Psalm 3:3

The eyes of the LORD run to and fro throughout the whole earth, to show Himself strong on behalf of those whose heart is loyal to Him.

2 Chronicles 16:9b

The LORD your God, who goes before you, He will fight for you, according to all He did for you in Egypt before your eyes.

Deuteronomy 1:30

But the Lord is faithful, who will establish you and guard you from the evil one.

2 Thessalonians 3:3

If you indeed obey His voice and do all that I speak, then I will be an enemy to your enemies and an adversary to your adversaries.

Exodus 23:22

He will guard the feet of His saints, but the wicked shall be silent in darkness. For by strength no man shall prevail.

1 Samuel 2:9

You have been a shelter for me, a strong tower from the enemy.

Psalm 61:3

The LORD your God in your midst,
The Mighty One, will save;
He will rejoice over you with gladness,
He will quiet you with His love,
He will rejoice over you with singing.

Zephaniah 3:17

A thousand may fall at your side, and ten thousand at your right hand; but it shall not come near you.

Psalm 91:7

The eyes of the LORD are on the righteous, and His ears are open to their prayers; but the face of the LORD is against those who do evil.

And who is he who will harm you if you become followers of what is good?

1 Peter 3:12, 13

The eternal God is your refuge, and underneath are the everlasting arms; He will thrust out the enemy from before you, and will say, "Destroy!"

Deuteronomy 33:27

So shall they fear the name of the LORD from the west, and His glory from the rising of the sun; when the enemy comes in like a flood, the Spirit of the LORD will lift up a standard against him.

Isaiah 59:19

Security 🕊

Blessed be the God and Father of our Lord Jesus Christ, who according to His abundant mercy has begotten us again to a living hope through the resurrection of Jesus Christ from the dead, to an inheritance incorruptible and undefiled and that does not fade away, reserved in heaven for you, who are kept by the power of God through faith for salvation ready to be revealed in the last time.

1 Peter 1:3–5

My sheep hear My voice, and I know them, and they follow Me.

And I give them eternal life, and they shall never perish; neither shall anyone snatch them out of My hand.

My Father, who has given them to Me, is greater than all; and no one is able to snatch them out of My Father's hand.

John 10:27–29

Being confident of this very thing, that He who has begun a good work in you will complete it until the day of Jesus Christ.

Philippians 1:6

I am persuaded that neither death nor life, nor angels nor principalities nor powers, nor things present nor things to come, nor height nor depth, nor any other created thing, shall be able to separate us from the love of God which is in Christ Jesus our Lord.

Romans 8:38, 39

All that the Father gives Me will come to Me, and the one who comes to Me I will by no means cast out.

John 6:37

Now to Him who is able to keep you from stumbling, and to present you faultless before the presence of His glory with exceeding joy, to God our Savior, who alone is wise, be glory and majesty, dominion and power, both now and forever. Amen.

Jude 24, 25

Lift up your eyes on high,
And see who has created these things,
Who brings out their host by number;
He calls them all by name,
By the greatness of His might
And the strength of His power;
Not one is missing.

Isaiah 40:26

Surely goodness and mercy shall follow me all the days of my life; and I will dwell in the house of the LORD forever.

Psalm 23:6

Do not labor for the food which perishes, but for the food which endures to everlasting life, which the Son of Man will give you, because God the Father has set His seal on Him.

John 6:27

Who also has sealed us and given us the Spirit in our hearts as a guarantee.

2 Corinthians 1:22

In Him you also trusted, after you heard the word of truth, the gospel of your salvation; in whom also, having believed, you were sealed with the Holy Spirit of promise.

Ephesians 1:13

Do not grieve the Holy Spirit of God, by whom you were sealed for the day of redemption.

Ephesians 4:30

Sufficiency 🕊

God is able to make all grace abound toward you, that you, always having all sufficiency in all things, may have an abundance for every good work.

2 Corinthians 9:8

My God shall supply all your need according to His riches in glory by Christ Jesus.

Philippians 4:19

Therefore I say to you, whatever things you ask when you pray, believe that you receive them, and you will have them.

Mark 11:24

Not that we are sufficient of ourselves to think of anything as being from ourselves, but our sufficiency is from God.

2 Corinthians 3:5

I can do all things through Christ who strengthens me.

Philippians 4:13

What is the exceeding greatness of His power toward us who believe, according to the working of His mighty power.

Ephesians 1:19

He said to me, "My grace is sufficient for you, for My strength is made perfect in weakness." Therefore most gladly I will rather boast in my infirmities, that the power of Christ may rest upon me.

2 Corinthians 12:9

Yet in all these things we are more than conquerors through Him who loved us.

Romans 8:37

Blessed be the God and Father of our Lord Jesus Christ, who has blessed us with every spiritual blessing in the heavenly places in Christ.

Ephesians 1:3

Whatever you ask in My name, that I will do, that the Father may be glorified in the Son.

John 14:13

In that day you will ask Me nothing. Most assuredly, I say to you, whatever you ask the Father in My name He will give you.

Until now you have asked nothing in My name. Ask, and you will receive, that your joy may be full.

John 16:23, 24

And whatever things you ask in prayer, believing, you will receive.

Matthew 21:22

He who did not spare His own Son, but delivered Him up for us all, how shall He not with Him also freely give us all things?

Romans 8:32

His divine power has given to us all things that pertain to life and godliness, through the knowledge of Him who called us by glory and virtue, by which have been given to us exceedingly great and precious promises, that through these you may be partakers of the divine nature, having escaped the corruption that is in the world through lust.

2 Peter 1:3, 4

Bless the LORD, O my soul,
And forget not all His benefits:
Who forgives all your iniquities,
Who heals all your diseases,
Who redeems your life from destruction,
Who crowns you with lovingkindness and
      tender mercies,

Psalm 103:2–4

Promises of Truth
from God's Word

Salvation by Faith ✎

If you confess with your mouth the Lord Jesus and believe in your heart that God has raised Him from the dead, you will be saved.

For with the heart one believes unto righteousness, and with the mouth confession is made unto salvation.

For the Scripture says, "Whoever believes on Him will not be put to shame."

Romans 10:9–11

Most assuredly, I say to you, he who hears My word and believes in Him who sent Me has everlasting life, and shall not come into judgment, but has passed from death into life.

John 5:24

You are all sons of God through faith in Christ Jesus.

For as many of you as were baptized into Christ have put on Christ.

There is neither Jew nor Greek, there is neither slave nor free, there is neither male nor female; for you are all one in Christ Jesus.

Galatians 3:26–28

If anyone is in Christ, he is a new creation; old things have passed away; behold, all things have become new.

2 Corinthians 5:17

Whoever confesses Me before men, him I will also confess before My Father who is in heaven.

And he who does not take his cross and follow after Me is not worthy of Me.

He who finds his life will lose it, and he who loses his life for My sake will find it.

Matthew 10:32, 38–39

I have been crucified with Christ; it is no longer I who live, but Christ lives in me; and the life which I now live in the flesh I live by faith in the Son of God, who loved me and gave Himself for me.

Galatians 2:20

Having been born again, not of corruptible seed but incorruptible, through the word of God which lives and abides forever.

1 Peter 1:23

We know that we have passed from death to life, because we love the brethren. He who does not love his brother abides in death.

1 John 3:14

Those who are Christ's have crucified the flesh with its passions and desires.

If we live in the Spirit, let us also walk in the Spirit.

Galatians 5:24–25

I will give you a new heart and put a new spirit within you; I will take the heart of stone out of your flesh and give you a heart of flesh.

I will put My Spirit within you and cause you to walk in My statutes, and you will keep My judgments and do them.

Ezekiel 36:26–27

He who received seed on the good ground is he who hears the word and understands it, who indeed bears fruit and produces: some a hundredfold, some sixty, some thirty.

Matthew 13:23

Knowing this, that our old man was crucified with Him, that the body of sin might be done away with, that we should no longer be slaves of sin.

For he who has died has been freed from sin.

Now if we died with Christ, we believe that we shall also live with Him.

Romans 6:6–8

God's Powerful Word ✦

All Scripture is given by inspiration of God, and is profitable for doctrine, for reproof, for correction, for instruction in righteousness.

2 Timothy 3:16

Knowing this first, that no prophecy of Scripture is of any private interpretation, for prophecy never came by the will of man, but holy men of God spoke as they were moved by the Holy Spirit.

2 Peter 1:20, 21

For the word of God is living and powerful, and sharper than any two-edged sword, piercing even to the division of soul and spirit, and of joints and marrow, and is a discerner of the thoughts and intents of the heart.

Hebrews 4:12

By the word of the LORD the heavens were made, and all the host of them by the breath of His mouth.

Psalm 33:6

Forever, O LORD, your word is settled in heaven.

Psalm 119:89

For as the rain comes down, and the snow
      from heaven,
And do not return there,
But water the earth,
And make it bring forth and bud,
That it may give seed to the sower
And bread to the eater,
So shall My word be that goes forth from
      My mouth;
It shall not return to Me void,
But it shall accomplish what I please,
And it shall prosper in the thing for which
      I sent it.

Isaiah 55:10, 11

You search the Scriptures, for in them you think you have eternal life; and these are they which testify of Me.

John 5:39

Having been born again, not of corruptible seed but incorruptible, through the word of God which lives and abides forever.

1 Peter 1:23

By the word of the LORD the heavens were made, and all the host of them by the breath of His mouth.

Psalm 33:6

He spoke, and it was done; He commanded, and it stood fast.

Psalm 33:9

Where is the wise? Where is the scribe? Where is the disputer of this age? Has not God made foolish the wisdom of this world?

1 Corinthians 1:20

"All flesh is as grass,
  And all the glory of man as the flower
    of the grass.
  The grass withers,
  And its flower falls away,
  But the word of the LORD endures
    forever."
Now this is the word which by the gospel
  was preached to you.

1 Peter 1:24, 25

Heaven and earth will pass away, but My words will by no means pass away.

Mark 13:31

The Holy Spirit ✒

Do you not know that your body is the temple of the Holy Spirit who is in you, whom you have from God, and you are not your own?

1 Corinthians 6:19

Now hope does not disappoint, because the love of God has been poured out in our hearts by the Holy Spirit who was given to us.

Romans 5:5

I will pray the Father, and He will give you another Helper, that He may abide with you forever—the Spirit of truth, whom the world cannot receive, because it neither sees Him nor knows Him; but you know Him, for He dwells with you and will be in you.

John 14:16, 17

If you then, being evil, know how to give good gifts to your children, how much more will your heavenly Father give the Holy Spirit to those who ask Him!

Luke 11:13

Nevertheless I tell you the truth. It is to your advantage that I go away; for if I do not go away, the Helper will not come to you; but if I depart, I will send Him to you.

However, when He, the Spirit of truth, has come, He will guide you into all truth; for He will not speak on His own authority, but whatever He hears He will speak; and He will tell you things to come.

John 16:7, 13

I indeed baptize you with water unto repentance, but He who is coming after me is mightier than I, whose sandals I am not worthy to carry. He will baptize you with the Holy Spirit and fire.

Matthew 3:11

"He who believes in Me, as the Scripture has said, out of his heart will flow rivers of living water."

But this He spoke concerning the Spirit, whom those believing in Him would receive; for the Holy Spirit was not yet given, because Jesus was not yet glorified.

John 7:38, 39

And it shall come to pass afterward
That I will pour out My Spirit on all flesh;
Your sons and your daughters shall
    prophesy,
Your old men shall dream dreams,
Your young men shall see visions.

Joel 2:28

And being assembled together with them, He commanded them not to depart from Jerusalem, but to wait for the Promise of the Father, "which," He said, "you have heard from Me; for John truly baptized with water, but you shall be baptized with the Holy Spirit not many days from now.

"But you shall receive power when the Holy Spirit has come upon you; and you shall be witnesses to Me in Jerusalem, and in all Judea and Samaria, and to the end of the earth."

Acts 1:4, 5, 8

They were all filled with the Holy Spirit and began to speak with other tongues, as the Spirit gave them utterance.

Acts 2:4

Then Peter said to them, "Repent, and let every one of you be baptized in the name of Jesus Christ for the remission of sins; and you shall receive the gift of the Holy Spirit."

Acts 2:38

The Church 🕊

That in the dispensation of the fullness of the times He might gather together in one all things in Christ, both which are in heaven and which are on earth—in Him.

And He put all things under His feet, and gave Him to be head over all things to the church, which is His body, the fullness of Him who fills all in all.

Ephesians 1:10, 22–23

He has delivered us from the power of darkness and conveyed us into the kingdom of the Son of His love, and He is the head of the body, the church, who is the beginning, the firstborn from the dead, that in all things He may have the preeminence.

Colossians 1:13, 18

Blessed be the LORD, who has given rest to His people Israel, according to all that He promised. There has not failed one word of all His good promise, which He promised through His servant Moses.

1 Kings 8:56

Your mercy, O LORD, is in the heavens; Your faithfulness reaches to the clouds.

Psalm 36:5

I will sing of the mercies of the LORD
    forever;
With my mouth will I make known Your
    faithfulness to all generations.
For I have said, "Mercy shall be built up
    forever;
Your faithfulness You shall establish in the
    very heavens."
Nevertheless My lovingkindness I will not
    utterly take from him,
Nor allow My faithfulness to fail.
My covenant I will not break,
Nor alter the word that has gone out of My
    lips.

Psalm 89:1, 2, 33, 34

He will not allow your foot to be moved;
He who keeps you will not slumber.
Behold, He who keeps Israel
Shall neither slumber nor sleep.

Psalm 121:3, 4

Till I come, give attention to reading, to
exhortation, to doctrine.

1 Timothy 4:13

He said to them, "But who do you say that I am?"

Simon Peter answered and said, "You are the Christ, the Son of the living God."

Jesus answered and said to him, "Blessed are you, Simon Bar-Jonah, for flesh and blood has not revealed this to you, but My Father who is in heaven.

"And I also say to you that you are Peter, and on this rock I will build My church, and the gates of Hades shall not prevail against it."

Matthew 16:15–18

Having been built on the foundation of the apostles and prophets, Jesus Christ Himself being the chief cornerstone, in whom the whole building, being joined together, grows into a holy temple in the Lord, in whom you also are being built together for a dwelling place of God in the Spirit.

Ephesians 2:20–22

From whom the whole family in heaven and earth is named, to Him be glory in the church by Christ Jesus to all generations, forever and ever.

Ephesians 3:15, 21

Stewardship ✒

Will a man rob God?
Yet you have robbed Me!
But you say,
"In what way have we robbed You?"
In tithes and offerings.
You are cursed with a curse,
For you have robbed Me,
Even this whole nation.
Bring all the tithes into the storehouse,
That there may be food in My house,
And try Me now in this,
Says the LORD of hosts,
If I will not open for you the windows
of heaven
And pour out for you such blessing
That there will not be room enough
to receive it.
And I will rebuke the devourer for
your sakes,
So that he will not destroy the fruit of
your ground,
Nor shall the vine fail to bear fruit for
you in the field.

Malachi 3:8–11

Now concerning the collection for the saints, as I have given orders to the churches of Galatia, so you must do also: On the first day of the week let each one of you lay something aside, storing up as he may prosper, that there be no collections when I come.

Corinthians 16:1, 2

But this I say: He who sows sparingly will also reap sparingly, and he who sows bountifully will also reap bountifully.

So let each one give as he purposes in his heart, not grudgingly or of necessity; for God loves a cheerful giver.

And God is able to make all grace abound toward you, that you, always having all sufficiency in all things, may have an abundance for every good work.

2 Corinthians 9:6–8

Whatever you do, do it heartily, as to the Lord and not to men, knowing that from the Lord you will receive the reward of the inheritance; for you serve the Lord Christ.

Colossians 3:23, 24

Lay up for yourselves treasures in heaven, where neither moth nor rust destroys and where thieves do not break in and steal.

For where your treasure is, there your heart will be also.

Matthew 6:20, 21

Give, and it will be given to you: good measure, pressed down, shaken together, and running over will be put into your bosom. For with the same measure that you use, it will be measured back to you.

Luke 6:38

Beloved, I pray that you may prosper in all things and be in health, just as your soul prospers.

3 John 2

But seek first the kingdom of God and His righteousness, and all these things shall be added to you.

Matthew 6:33

Heal the sick, cleanse the lepers, raise the dead, cast out demons. Freely you have received, freely give.

Matthew 10:8

Everyone who has left houses or brothers or sisters or father or mother or wife or children or lands, for My name's sake, shall receive a hundredfold, and inherit eternal life.

Matthew 19:29

Forsake foolishness and live,
And go in the way of understanding.
The fear of the LORD is the beginning
    of wisdom,
And the knowledge of the Holy One
    is understanding.

Proverbs 9:6, 10

Always pursue what is good both for yourselves and for all.

1 Thessalonians 5:15

Satan 🕊

Put on the whole armor of God, that you may be able to stand against the wiles of the devil.

For we do not wrestle against flesh and blood, but against principalities, against powers, against the rulers of the darkness of this age, against spiritual hosts of wickedness in the heavenly places.

Therefore take up the whole armor of God, that you may be able to withstand in the evil day, and having done all, to stand.

Stand therefore, having girded your waist with truth, having put on the breastplate of righteousness, and having shod your feet with the preparation of the gospel of peace; above all, taking the shield of faith with which you will be able to quench all the fiery darts of the wicked one.

And take the helmet of salvation, and the sword of the Spirit, which is the word of God; praying always with all prayer and supplication in the Spirit, being watchful to this end with all perseverance and supplication for all the saints.

Ephesians 6:10–18

Be sober, be vigilant; because your adversary the devil walks about like a roaring lion, seeking whom he may devour.

Resist him, steadfast in the faith, knowing that the same sufferings are experienced by your brotherhood in the world.

1 Peter 5:8, 9

Submit to God. Resist the devil and he will flee from you.

James 4:7

We see Jesus, who was made a little lower than the angels, for the suffering of death crowned with glory and honor, that He, by the grace of God, might taste death for everyone.

Inasmuch then as the children have partaken of flesh and blood, He Himself likewise shared in the same, that through death He might destroy him who had the power of death, that is, the devil, and release those who through fear of death were all their lifetime subject to bondage.

Hebrews 2:9, 14, 15

Then the seventy returned with joy, saying, "Lord, even the demons are subject to us in Your name."

And He said to them, "I saw Satan fall like lightning from heaven. Behold, I give you the authority to trample on serpents and scorpions, and over all the power of the enemy, and nothing shall by any means hurt you."

Luke 10:17–19

These signs will follow those who believe: In My name they will cast out demons; they will speak with new tongues; they will take up serpents; and if they drink anything deadly, it will by no means hurt them; they will lay hands on the sick, and they will recover.

Mark 16:17, 18

If I cast out demons by the Spirit of God, surely the kingdom of God has come upon you.

Or how can one enter a strong man's house and plunder his goods, unless he first binds the strong man? And then he will plunder his house.

Matthew 12:28, 29

Christ's Return ✈

But I do not want you to be ignorant, brethren, concerning those who have fallen asleep, lest you sorrow as others who have no hope.

For if we believe that Jesus died and rose again, even so God will bring with Him those who sleep in Jesus.

For this we say to you by the word of the Lord, that we who are alive and remain until the coming of the Lord will by no means precede those who are asleep.

For the Lord Himself will descend from heaven with a shout, with the voice of an archangel, and with the trumpet of God. And the dead in Christ will rise first.

Then we who are alive and remain shall be caught up together with them in the clouds to meet the Lord in the air. And thus we shall always be with the Lord.

Therefore comfort one another with these words.

1 Thessalonians 4:13–18

Looking for the blessed hope and glorious appearing of our great God and Savior Jesus Christ.

Titus 2:13

Who also said, "Men of Galilee, why do you stand gazing up into heaven? This same Jesus, who was taken up from you into heaven, will so come in like manner as you saw Him go into heaven."

Acts 1:11

Beloved, now we are children of God; and it has not yet been revealed what we shall be, but we know that when He is revealed, we shall be like Him, for we shall see Him as He is.

And everyone who has this hope in Him purifies himself, just as He is pure.

1 John 3:2, 3

And there will be signs in the sun, in the moon, and in the stars; and on the earth distress of nations, with perplexity, the sea and the waves roaring; men's hearts failing them from fear and the expectation of those things which are coming on the earth, for the powers of heaven will be shaken.

Then they will see the Son of Man coming in a cloud with power and great glory.

Now when these things begin to happen, look up and lift up your heads, because your redemption draws near.

Luke 21:25–28

There is laid up for me the crown of right-eousness, which the Lord, the righteous Judge, will give to me on that Day, and not to me only but also to all who have loved His appearing.

2 Timothy 4:8

So you also, when you see all these things, know that it is near—at the doors!

Matthew 24:33

Let not your heart be troubled; you believe in God, believe also in Me.

In My Father's house are many mansions; if it were not so, I would have told you. I go to prepare a place for you.

And if I go and prepare a place for you, I will come again and receive you to Myself; that where I am, there you may be also.

And where I go you know, and the way you know.

John 14:1–4

Let us hold fast the confession of our hope without wavering, for He who promised is faithful.

Hebrews 10:23

If then you were raised with Christ, seek those things which are above, where Christ is, sitting at the right hand of God. Set your mind on things above, not on things on the earth. For you died, and your life is hidden with Christ in God. When Christ who is our life appears, then you also will appear with Him in glory.

Colossians 3:1–4

All the ends of the world
Shall remember and turn to the LORD,
And all the families of the nations
Shall worship before You.
For the kingdom is the LORD's,
And He rules over the nations.

Psalm 22:27–28

Promises About
Christian Growth

Committing Your Life to Christ ✒

That if you confess with your mouth the Lord Jesus and believe in your heart that God has raised Him from the dead, you will be saved.

For with the heart one believes unto righteousness, and with the mouth confession is made unto salvation.

For the Scripture says, "Whoever believes on Him will not be put to shame."

For there is no distinction between Jew and Greek, for the same Lord over all is rich to all who call upon Him.

For "whoever calls on the name of the LORD shall be saved."

Romans 10:9–13

Seek the LORD while He may be found,
Call upon Him while He is near.
Let the wicked forsake his way,
And the unrighteous man his thoughts;
Let him return to the LORD,
And He will have mercy on him;
And to our God,
For He will abundantly pardon.

Isaiah 55:6–7

Behold, I stand at the door and knock. If anyone hears My voice and opens the door, I will come in to him and dine with him, and he with Me.

Revelation 3:20

All that the Father gives Me will come to Me, and the one who comes to Me I will by no means cast out.

And this is the will of Him who sent Me, that everyone who sees the Son and believes in Him may have everlasting life; and I will raise him up at the last day.

No one can come to Me unless the Father who sent Me draws him; and I will raise him up at the last day.

It is written in the prophets, "And they shall all be taught by God." Therefore everyone who has heard and learned from the Father comes to Me.

Not that anyone has seen the Father, except He who is from God; He has seen the Father.

Most assuredly, I say to you, he who believes in Me has everlasting life.

John 6:37, 40, 44–47

Without faith it is impossible to please Him, for he who comes to God must believe that He is, and that He is a rewarder of those who diligently seek Him.

Hebrews 11:6

The Lord is not slack concerning His promise, as some count slackness, but is longsuffering toward us, not willing that any should perish but that all should come to repentance.

But grow in the grace and knowledge of our Lord and Savior Jesus Christ. To Him be the glory both now and forever. Amen.

2 Peter 3:9, 18

Having been set free from sin, and having become slaves of God, you have your fruit to holiness, and the end, everlasting life.

For the wages of sin is death, but the gift of God is eternal life in Christ Jesus our Lord.

Romans 6:22–23

Come now, you who say, "Today or tomorrow we will go to such and such a city, spend a year there, buy and sell, and make a profit"; whereas you do not know what will happen tomorrow. For what is your life? It is even a vapor that appears for a little time and then vanishes away.

Instead you ought to say, "If the Lord wills, we shall live and do this or that."

James 4:13–15

Beware of false prophets, who come to you in sheep's clothing, but inwardly they are ravenous wolves.

You will know them by their fruits. Do men gather grapes from thornbushes or figs from thistles?

Even so, every good tree bears good fruit, but a bad tree bears bad fruit.

Therefore by their fruits you will know them.

Not everyone who says to Me, "Lord, Lord," shall enter the kingdom of heaven, but he who does the will of My Father in heaven.

Many will say to Me in that day, "Lord, Lord, have we not prophesied in Your name, cast out demons in Your name, and done many wonders in Your name?"

And then I will declare to them, "I never knew you; depart from Me, you who practice lawlessness!"

Matthew 7:15–17, 20–23

They profess to know God, but in works they deny Him, being abominable, disobedient, and disqualified for every good work.

Titus 1:16

Beloved, do not believe every spirit, but test the spirits, whether they are of God; because many false prophets have gone out into the world.

By this you know the Spirit of God: Every spirit that confesses that Jesus Christ has come in the flesh is of God, and every spirit that does not confess that Jesus Christ has come in the flesh is not of God. And this is the spirit of the Antichrist, which you have heard was coming, and is now already in the world.

1 John 4:1–3

And when they say to you, "Seek those who are mediums and wizards, who whisper and mutter," should not a people seek their God? Should they seek the dead on behalf of the living?

To the law and to the testimony! If they do not speak according to this word, it is because there is no light in them.

Isaiah 8:19–20

Stand fast therefore in the liberty by which Christ has made us free, and do not be entangled again with a yoke of bondage.

Galatians 5:1

"Behold, I am against those who prophesy false dreams," says the LORD, "and tell them, and cause My people to err by their lies and by their recklessness. Yet I did not send them or command them; therefore they shall not profit this people at all," says the LORD.

Jeremiah 23:32

A good tree does not bear bad fruit, nor does a bad tree bear good fruit.

For every tree is known by its own fruit. For men do not gather figs from thorns, nor do they gather grapes from a bramble bush.

Luke 6:43–44

For God is not the author of confusion but of peace, as in all the churches of the saints.

1 Corinthians 14:33

God has not given us a spirit of fear, but of power and of love and of a sound mind.

2 Timothy 1:7

He who sins is of the devil, for the devil has sinned from the beginning. For this purpose the Son of God was manifested, that He might destroy the works of the devil.

1 John 3:8

Standing Against Worldliness ✒

No one can serve two masters; for either he will hate the one and love the other, or else he will be loyal to the one and despise the other. You cannot serve God and mammon.

Matthew 6:24

Do not love the world or the things in the world. If anyone loves the world, the love of the Father is not in him.

For all that is in the world—the lust of the flesh, the lust of the eyes, and the pride of life—is not of the Father but is of the world.

And the world is passing away, and the lust of it; but he who does the will of God abides forever.

1 John 2:15–17

Do not be conformed to this world, but be transformed by the renewing of your mind, that you may prove what is that good and acceptable and perfect will of God.

Romans 12:2

Have no fellowship with the unfruitful works of darkness, but rather expose them.

Ephesians 5:11

And do this, knowing the time, that now it is high time to awake out of sleep; for now our salvation is nearer than when we first believed.

The night is far spent, the day is at hand. Therefore let us cast off the works of darkness, and let us put on the armor of light.

Let us walk properly, as in the day, not in revelry and drunkenness, not in lewdness and lust, not in strife and envy.

But put on the Lord Jesus Christ, and make no provision for the flesh, to fulfill its lusts.

Romans 13:11–14

The Lord knows how to deliver the godly out of temptations and to reserve the unjust under punishment for the day of judgment.

2 Peter 2:9

Then He said to them all, "If anyone desires to come after Me, let him deny himself, and take up his cross daily, and follow Me.

"For whoever desires to save his life will lose it, but whoever loses his life for My sake will save it.

"For what profit is it to a man if he gains the whole world, and is himself destroyed or lost?"

Luke 9:23–25

Now therefore, fear the LORD, serve Him in sincerity and in truth, and put away the gods which your fathers served on the other side of the River and in Egypt. Serve the LORD!

Joshua 24:14

Choosing rather to suffer affliction with the people of God than to enjoy the passing pleasures of sin, esteeming the reproach of Christ greater riches than the treasures in Egypt; for he looked to the reward.

By faith he forsook Egypt, not fearing the wrath of the king; for he endured as seeing Him who is invisible.

Hebrews 11:25–27

By which have been given to us exceedingly great and precious promises, that through these you may be partakers of the divine nature, having escaped the corruption that is in the world through lust.

2 Peter 1:4

Take heed to yourselves, lest your hearts be weighed down with carousing, drunkenness, and cares of this life, and that Day come on you un-expectedly.

Luke 21:34

Overcoming Lust ✒

Do you not know that your bodies are members of Christ? Shall I then take the members of Christ and make them members of a harlot? Certainly not!

Or do you not know that he who is joined to a harlot is one body with her? For "the two," He says, "shall become one flesh."

But he who is joined to the Lord is one spirit with Him.

Flee sexual immorality. Every sin that a man does is outside the body, but he who commits sexual immorality sins against his own body.

Or do you not know that your body is the temple of the Holy Spirit who is in you, whom you have from God, and you are not your own?

For you were bought at a price; therefore glorify God in your body and in your spirit, which are God's.

1 Corinthians 6:15–20

I say then: Walk in the Spirit, and you shall not fulfill the lust of the flesh.

For the flesh lusts against the Spirit, and the Spirit against the flesh; and these are contrary to one another, so that you do not do the things that you wish.

Galatians 5:16–17

No temptation has overtaken you except such as is common to man; but God is faithful, who will not allow you to be tempted beyond what you are able, but with the temptation will also make the way of escape, that you may be able to bear it.

1 Corinthians 10:13

Put off, concerning your former conduct, the old man which grows corrupt according to the deceitful lusts, and be renewed in the spirit of your mind, and . . . put on the new man which was created according to God, in true righteousness and holiness . . . nor give place to the devil.

Ephesians 4:22–24, 27

Now therefore, listen to me, my children;
Pay attention to the words of my mouth:
Do not let your heart turn aside to
    her ways,
Do not stray into her paths;
For she has cast down many wounded,
And all who were slain by her were
    strong men.
Her house is the way to hell,
Descending to the chambers of death.

Proverbs 7:24–27

The Lord knows how to deliver the godly out of temptations and to reserve the unjust under punishment for the day of judgment.

2 Peter 2:9

My brethren, count it all joy when you fall into various trials, knowing that the testing of your faith produces patience.

But let patience have its perfect work, that you may be perfect and complete, lacking nothing.

James 1:2–4

Do not lust after her beauty in your heart,
Nor let her allure you with her eyelids.
For by means of a harlot
A man is reduced to a crust of bread;
And an adulteress will prey upon his
    precious life.

Proverbs 6:25–26

Likewise you also, reckon yourselves to be dead indeed to sin, but alive to God in Christ Jesus our Lord.

Therefore do not let sin reign in your mortal body, that you should obey it in its lusts.

Romans 6:11–12

Submit to God. Resist the devil and he will flee from you.

James 4:7

I say then: Walk in the Spirit, and you shall not fulfill the lust of the flesh. For the flesh lusts against the Spirit, and the Spirit against the flesh; and these are contrary to one another, so that you do not do the things that you wish.

Galatians 5:16–17

Each one is tempted when he is drawn away by his own desires and enticed. Then, when desire has conceived, it gives birth to sin; and sin, when it is full-grown, brings forth death.

Do not be deceived, my beloved brethren.

James 1:14–16

Setting Aside Pride ✒

Pride goes before destruction,
And a haughty spirit before a fall.
Better to be of a humble spirit with the
     lowly,
Than to divide the spoil with the proud.
He who heeds the word wisely will
     find good,
And whoever trusts in the LORD,
     happy is he.

Proverbs 16:18–20

He who is of a proud heart stirs up strife,
But he who trusts in the LORD will
     be prospered.
He who trusts in his own heart is a fool,
But whoever walks wisely will be delivered.

Proverbs 28:25–26

Then Jesus called a little child to Him, set him in the midst of them, and said, "Assuredly, I say to you, unless you are converted and become as little children, you will by no means enter the kingdom of heaven. Therefore whoever humbles himself as this little child is the greatest in the kingdom of heaven."

Matthew 18:2–4

But He gives more grace. Therefore He says: "God resists the proud, but gives grace to the humble."

Therefore submit to God. Resist the devil and he will flee from you.

Humble yourselves in the sight of the Lord, and He will lift you up.

James 4:6–7, 10

Yet it shall not be so among you; but whoever desires to become great among you, let him be your servant

And whoever desires to be first among you, let him be your slave.

Matthew 20:26–27

Likewise you younger people, submit yourselves to your elders. Yes, all of you be submissive to one another, and be clothed with humility, for "God resists the proud, but gives grace to the humble."

Therefore humble yourselves under the mighty hand of God, that He may exalt you in due time.

1 Peter 5:5–6

But we have this treasure in earthen vessels, that the excellence of the power may be of God and not of us.

2 Corinthians 4:7

Hear and give ear:
Do not be proud,
For the LORD has spoken.
Give glory to the LORD your God
Before He causes darkness,
And before your feet stumble
On the dark mountains,
And while you are looking for light,
He turns it into the shadow of death
And makes it dense darkness.
But if you will not hear it,
My soul will weep in secret for your pride;
My eyes will weep bitterly
And run down with tears,
Because the LORD's flock has been
    taken captive.

Jeremiah 13:15–17

Take My yoke upon you and learn from Me,
for I am gentle and lowly in heart, and you will
find rest for your souls.
For My yoke is easy and My burden is light.
Matthew 11:29–30

The fear of the LORD is the instruction of
wisdom, and before honor is humility.
Proverbs 15:33

Choosing to Speak Carefully ✒

Death and life are in the power of the tongue, and those who love it will eat its fruit.

Proverbs 18:21

Let no corrupt word proceed out of your mouth, but what is good for necessary edification, that it may impart grace to the hearers.

Let all bitterness, wrath, anger, clamor, and evil speaking be put away from you, with all malice.

And be kind to one another, tenderhearted, forgiving one another, just as God in Christ forgave you.

Ephesians 4:29, 31–32

Pleasant words are like a honeycomb, sweetness to the soul and health to the bones.

Proverbs 16:24

He who guards his mouth preserves his life, But he who opens wide his lips shall have destruction.

Proverbs 13:3

A good man out of the good treasure of his heart brings forth good; and an evil man out of the evil treasure of his heart brings forth evil. For out of the abundance of the heart his mouth speaks.

Luke 6:45

But I say to you that for every idle word men may speak, they will give account of it in the day of judgment.

Matthew 12:36

Sing to Him, sing psalms to Him; talk of all His wondrous works!

1 Chronicles 16:9

Whoever guards his mouth and tongue keeps his soul from troubles.

Proverbs 21:23

Do not be a witness against your neighbor without cause, for would you deceive with your lips?

Proverbs 24:28

Avoid foolish disputes, genealogies, contentions, and strivings about the law; for they are unprofitable and useless.

Titus 3:9

O Timothy! Guard what was committed to your trust, avoiding the profane and idle babblings and contradictions of what is falsely called knowledge—by professing it some have strayed concerning the faith. Grace be with you. Amen.

1 Timothy 6:20–21

As long as my breath is in me,
And the breath of God in my nostrils,
My lips will not speak wickedness,
Nor my tongue utter deceit.

Job 27:3–4

As He who called you is holy, you also be holy in all your conduct.

1 Peter 1:15

Who, when He was reviled, did not revile in return; when He suffered, He did not threaten, but committed Himself to Him who judges righteously.

1 Peter 2:23

He who would love life and see good days, let him refrain his tongue from evil, and his lips from speaking deceit.

1 Peter 3:10

Keeping Centered in Christ ✈

Let the word of Christ dwell in you richly in all wisdom, teaching and admonishing one another in psalms and hymns and spiritual songs, singing with grace in your hearts to the Lord.

And whatever you do in word or deed, do all in the name of the Lord Jesus, giving thanks to God the Father through Him.

Colossians 3:16–17

I love those who love me, and those who seek me diligently will find me.

Proverbs 8:17

Seek the LORD and His strength;
Seek His face evermore!
Remember His marvelous works which
 He has done,
His wonders, and the judgments
 of His mouth,

1 Chronicles 16:11–12

Trust in Him at all times, you people; pour out your heart before Him; God is a refuge for us.

Psalm 62:8

You are My friends if you do whatever I command you.

No longer do I call you servants, for a servant does not know what his master is doing; but I have called you friends, for all things that I heard from My Father I have made known to you.

You did not choose Me, but I chose you and appointed you that you should go and bear fruit, and that your fruit should remain, that whatever you ask the Father in My name He may give you.

John 15:14–16

Speaking to one another in psalms and hymns and spiritual songs, singing and making melody in your heart to the Lord, giving thanks always for all things to God the Father in the name of our Lord Jesus Christ.

Ephesians 5:19–20

I will bless the LORD at all times;
His praise shall continually be in
my mouth.
My soul shall make its boast in the LORD;
The humble shall hear of it and be glad.
Oh, magnify the LORD with me,
And let us exalt His name together.
I sought the LORD, and He heard me,
And delivered me from all my fears.

Psalm 34:1–4

Truly my soul silently waits for God;
From Him comes my salvation.
He only is my rock and my salvation;
He is my defense;
I shall not be greatly moved.
My soul, wait silently for God alone,
For my expectation is from Him.
He only is my rock and my salvation;
He is my defense;
I shall not be moved.
In God is my salvation and my glory;
The rock of my strength,
And my refuge, is in God.

Psalm 62:1–2, 5–7

Put on the Lord Jesus Christ, and make no
provision for the flesh, to fulfill its lusts.

Romans 13:14

In You, O LORD, I put my trust;
Let me never be put to shame.
For You are my hope, O Lord GOD;
You are my trust from my youth.
Let my mouth be filled with Your praise
And with Your glory all the day.

Psalm 71:1, 5, 8

"Am I a God near at hand," says the LORD,
"And not a God afar off?
  Can anyone hide himself in secret places,
  So I shall not see him?" says the LORD;
"Do I not fill heaven and earth?" says
      the LORD.

Jeremiah 23:23–24

For of Him and through Him and to Him
are all things, to whom be glory forever.

Romans 11:36

Promises to Help
You Serve God

Praying Effectively 🕊

Be anxious for nothing, but in everything by prayer and supplication, with thanksgiving, let your requests be made known to God; and the peace of God, which surpasses all understanding, will guard your hearts and minds through Christ Jesus.

Philippians 4:6–7

Assuredly, I say to you, whatever you bind on earth will be bound in heaven, and whatever you loose on earth will be loosed in heaven.

Again I say to you that if two of you agree on earth concerning anything that they ask, it will be done for them by My Father in heaven.

Matthew 18:18–19

Let us therefore come boldly to the throne of grace, that we may obtain mercy and find grace to help in time of need.

Hebrews 4:16

Without faith it is impossible to please Him, for he who comes to God must believe that He is, and that He is a rewarder of those who diligently seek Him.

Hebrews 11:6

Confess your trespasses to one another, and pray for one another, that you may be healed. The effective, fervent prayer of a righteous man avails much.

Elijah was a man with a nature like ours, and he prayed earnestly that it would not rain; and it did not rain on the land for three years and six months.

And he prayed again, and the heaven gave rain, and the earth produced its fruit.

James 5:16–18

Now in the morning, having risen a long while before daylight, He went out and departed to a solitary place; and there He prayed.

Mark 1:35

Now it came to pass in those days that He went out to the mountain to pray, and continued all night in prayer to God.

Luke 6:12

LORD, I cry out to You;
Make haste to me!
Give ear to my voice when I cry out
    to You.
Let my prayer be set before You as incense,
The lifting up of my hands as the evening
    sacrifice.

Psalm 141:1–2

So shall My word be that goes forth from My mouth; it shall not return to Me void, but it shall accomplish what I please, and it shall prosper in the thing for which I sent it.

Isaiah 55:11

So I say to you, ask, and it will be given to you; seek, and you will find; knock, and it will be opened to you.

Luke 11:9

When you pray, you shall not be like the hypocrites. For they love to pray standing in the synagogues and on the corners of the streets, that they may be seen by men. Assuredly, I say to you, they have their reward.

But you, when you pray, go into your room, and when you have shut your door, pray to your Father who is in the secret place; and your Father who sees in secret will reward you openly.

Matthew 6:5–6

Then He spoke a parable to them, that men always ought to pray and not lose heart.

Luke 18:1

For the eyes of the LORD are on the
    righteous,
And His ears are open to their prayers;
But the face of the LORD is against those
    who do evil.

1 Peter 3:12

Evening and morning and at noon I will
pray, and cry aloud, and He shall hear my voice.

Psalm 55:17

The LORD is far from the wicked,
But He hears the prayer of the righteous.

Proverbs 15:29

Pray without ceasing.

1 Thessalonians 5:17

Witnessing Effectively ✒

You are the light of the world. A city that is set on a hill cannot be hidden.

Nor do they light a lamp and put it under a basket, but on a lampstand, and it gives light to all who are in the house.

Let your light so shine before men, that they may see your good works and glorify your Father in heaven.

Matthew 5:14–16

No one, when he has lit a lamp, puts it in a secret place or under a basket, but on a lampstand, that those who come in may see the light.

Luke 11:33

Therefore settle it in your hearts not to meditate beforehand on what you will answer; for I will give you a mouth and wisdom which all your adversaries will not be able to contradict or resist.

Luke 21:14–15

But that the world may know that I love the Father, and as the Father gave Me commandment, so I do. Arise, let us go from here.

John 14:31

Praying always with all prayer and supplication in the Spirit, being watchful to this end with all perseverance and supplication for all the saints—and for me, that utterance may be given to me, that I may open my mouth boldly to make known the mystery of the gospel, for which I am an ambassador in chains; that in it I may speak boldly, as I ought to speak.

Ephesians 6:18–20

Finally, all of you be of one mind, having compassion for one another; love as brothers, be tenderhearted, be courteous; not returning evil for evil or reviling for reviling, but on the contrary blessing, knowing that you were called to this, that you may inherit a blessing.

For "He who would love life and see good days, let him refrain his tongue from evil, and his lips from speaking deceit.

Let him turn away from evil and do good; let him seek peace and pursue it.

But sanctify the Lord God in your hearts, and always be ready to give a defense to everyone who asks you a reason for the hope that is in you, with meekness and fear.

1 Peter 3:8–11, 15

Also I say to you, whoever confesses Me before men, him the Son of Man also will confess before the angels of God.

But he who denies Me before men will be denied before the angels of God.

Luke 12:8–9

Therefore do not be ashamed of the testimony of our Lord, nor of me His prisoner, but share with me in the sufferings for the gospel according to the power of God, who has saved us and called us with a holy calling, not according to our works, but according to His own purpose and grace which was given to us in Christ Jesus before time began, but has now been revealed by the appearing of our Savior Jesus Christ, who has abolished death and brought life and immortality to light through the gospel.

2 Timothy 1:8–10

The fruit of the righteous is a tree of life,
And he who wins souls is wise.

Proverbs 11:30

I will sing to the LORD as long as I live;
I will sing praise to my God while I have
my being.

Psalm 104:33

Understanding God's Will 🕊

The LORD will guide you continually,
And satisfy your soul in drought,
And strengthen your bones;
You shall be like a watered garden,
And like a spring of water, whose waters
    do not fail.

Isaiah 58:11

I say to you that likewise there will be more joy in heaven over one sinner who repents than over ninety-nine just persons who need no repentance.

Luke 15:7

"For My thoughts are not your thoughts,
    Nor are your ways My ways," says the
        LORD.
"For as the heavens are higher than the
        earth,
    So are My ways higher than your ways,
    And My thoughts than your thoughts."

Isaiah 55:8–9

Beloved, do not believe every spirit, but test the spirits, whether they are of God; because many false prophets have gone out into the world.

1 John 4:1

The Lord is not slack concerning His promise, as some count slackness, but is longsuffering toward us, not willing that any should perish but that all should come to repentance.

2 Peter 3:9

The Son of Man has come to save that which was lost.

Matthew 18:11

The spirit of a man is the lamp of the LORD, searching all the inner depths of his heart.

Proverbs 20:27

He found him in a desert land
And in the wasteland, a howling
      wilderness;
He encircled him, He instructed him,
He kept him as the apple of His eye.
As an eagle stirs up its nest,
Hovers over its young,
Spreading out its wings, taking them up,
Carrying them on its wings,
So the LORD alone led him,
And there was no foreign god with him.

Deuteronomy 32:10–12

So he shepherded them according to the integrity of his heart, and guided them by the skillfulness of his hands.

Psalm 78:72

You shall not go out with haste,
Nor go by flight;
For the LORD will go before you,
And the God of Israel will be your
    rear guard.

Isaiah 52:12

There are three that bear witness in heaven:
the Father, the Word, and the Holy Spirit; and
these three are one.

1 John 5:7

A man's heart plans his way,
But the LORD directs his steps.
The lot is cast into the lap,
But its every decision is from the LORD.

Proverbs 16:9, 33

God has not given us a spirit of fear, but of
power and of love and of a sound mind.

2 Timothy 1:7

Obeying God 🕊

That all the peoples of the earth may know that the LORD is God; there is no other.

Let your heart therefore be loyal to the LORD our God, to walk in His statutes and keep His commandments, as at this day.

1 Kings 8:60–61

Be doers of the word, and not hearers only, deceiving yourselves.

James 1:22

Now therefore, if you will indeed obey My voice and keep My covenant, then you shall be a special treasure to Me above all people; for all the earth is Mine.

Exodus 19:5

Do not be deceived, God is not mocked; for whatever a man sows, that he will also reap.

For he who sows to his flesh will of the flesh reap corruption, but he who sows to the Spirit will of the Spirit reap everlasting life.

Galatians 6:7–8

If you love Me, keep My commandments.

John 14:15

But Peter and the other apostles answered and said: "We ought to obey God rather than men."

Acts 5:29

I discipline my body and bring it into subjection, lest, when I have preached to others, I myself should become disqualified.

1 Corinthians 9:27

Casting down arguments and every high thing that exalts itself against the knowledge of God, bringing every thought into captivity to the obedience of Christ.

2 Corinthians 10:5

Whoever has no rule over his own spirit is like a city broken down, without walls.

Proverbs 25:28

He who is faithful in what is least is faithful also in much; and he who is unjust in what is least is unjust also in much.

Luke 16:10

Behold, You desire truth in the inward parts, and in the hidden part You will make me to know wisdom.

Psalm 51:6

The world is passing away, and the lust of it; but he who does the will of God abides forever.

1 John 2:17

If anyone does not abide in Me, he is cast out as a branch and is withered; and they gather them and throw them into the fire, and they are burned.

If you abide in Me, and My words abide in you, you will ask what you desire, and it shall be done for you.

If you keep My commandments, you will abide in My love, just as I have kept My Father's commandments and abide in His love.

John 15:6–7, 10

Now the just shall live by faith; but if any-one draws back, My soul has no pleasure in him.

Hebrews 10:38

Then Samuel said:
Has the LORD as great delight in burnt
    offerings and sacrifices,
As in obeying the voice of the LORD?
Behold, to obey is better than sacrifice,
And to heed than the fat of rams.

1 Samuel 15:22

Giving to God's Work ✒

Do not lay up for yourselves treasures on earth, where moth and rust destroy and where thieves break in and steal; but lay up for yourselves treasures in heaven, where neither moth nor rust destroys and where thieves do not break in and steal.

For where your treasure is, there your heart will be also.

Matthew 6:19–21

Now Jesus sat opposite the treasury and saw how the people put money into the treasury. And many who were rich put in much.

Then one poor widow came and threw in two mites, which make a quadrans.

So He called His disciples to Himself and said to them, "Assuredly, I say to you that this poor widow has put in more than all those who have given to the treasury; for they all put in out of their abundance, but she out of her poverty put in all that she had, her whole livelihood."

Mark 12:41–44

Give to the LORD the glory due His name; bring an offering, and come into His courts.

Psalm 96:8

But this I say: He who sows sparingly will also reap sparingly, and he who sows bountifully will also reap bountifully.

So let each one give as he purposes in his heart, not grudgingly or of necessity; for God loves a cheerful giver.

2 Corinthians 9:6–7

But woe to you Pharisees! For you tithe mint and rue and all manner of herbs, and pass by justice and the love of God. These you ought to have done, without leaving the others undone.

Luke 11:42

He who is faithful in what is least is faithful also in much; and he who is unjust in what is least is unjust also in much.

Therefore if you have not been faithful in the unrighteous mammon, who will commit to your trust the true riches?

Luke 16:10–11

He who has a generous eye will be blessed, for he gives of his bread to the poor.

Proverbs 22:9

Therefore bear fruits worthy of repentance, and do not think to say to yourselves, "We have Abraham as our father." For I say to you that God is able to raise up children to Abraham from these stones.

Matthew 3:8–9

Does he thank that servant because he did the things that were commanded him? I think not.

So likewise you, when you have done all those things which you are commanded, say, "We are unprofitable servants. We have done what was our duty to do."

Luke 17:9–10

As soon as the commandment was circulated, the children of Israel brought in abundance the firstfruits of grain and wine, oil and honey, and of all the produce of the field; and they brought in abundantly the tithe of everything.

2 Chronicles 31:5

Reading God's Word ✐

The word of God is living and powerful, and sharper than any two-edged sword, piercing even to the division of soul and spirit, and of joints and marrow, and is a discerner of the thoughts and intents of the heart.

Hebrews 4:12

By the word of the LORD the heavens were made, and all the host of them by the breath of His mouth.

Psalm 33:6

Your word I have hidden in my heart, that I might not sin against You!

I will delight myself in Your statutes; I will not forget Your word.

Psalm 119:11, 16

How sweet are Your words to my taste,
Sweeter than honey to my mouth!
Through Your precepts I get
    understanding;
Therefore I hate every false way.
Your word is a lamp to my feet
And a light to my path.

Psalm 119:103–105

Forever, O LORD,
Your word is settled in heaven.
Your faithfulness endures to all generations;
You established the earth, and it abides.

Psalm 119:89–90

Your testimonies are wonderful;
Therefore my soul keeps them.
The entrance of Your words gives light;
It gives understanding to the simple.

Psalm 119:29–30

As newborn babes, desire the pure milk of the word, that you may grow thereby, if indeed you have tasted that the Lord is gracious.

1 Peter 2:2–3

You are already clean because of the word which I have spoken to you.

John 15:3

The grass withers, the flower fades, but the word of our God stands forever.

Isaiah 40:8

He answered and said, "It is written, 'Man shall not live by bread alone, but by every word that proceeds from the mouth of God.' "

Matthew 4:4

Having been born again, not of corruptible seed but incorruptible, through the word of God which lives and abides forever, because "All flesh is as grass, and all the glory of man as the flower of the grass. The grass withers, and its flower falls away, but the word of the LORD endures forever."

Now this is the word which by the gospel was preached to you.

1 Peter 1:23–25

Heaven and earth will pass away, but My words will by no means pass away.

Luke 21:33

It is the Spirit who gives life; the flesh profits nothing. The words that I speak to you are spirit, and they are life.

John 6:63

Then Jesus said to those Jews who believed Him, "If you abide in My word, you are My disciples indeed.

"And you shall know the truth, and the truth shall make you free."

John 8:31–32

Walking with Christ 🕊

Abide in Me, and I in you. As the branch cannot bear fruit of itself, unless it abides in the vine, neither can you, unless you abide in Me.

I am the vine, you are the branches. He who abides in Me, and I in him, bears much fruit; for without Me you can do nothing.

If anyone does not abide in Me, he is cast out as a branch and is withered; and they gather them and throw them into the fire, and they are burned.

If you abide in Me, and My words abide in you, you will ask what you desire, and it shall be done for you.

John 15:4–7

And now, little children, abide in Him, that when He appears, we may have confidence and not be ashamed before Him at His coming.

1 John 2:28

I love those who love me, and those who seek me diligently will find me.

Proverbs 8:17

I will meditate on Your precepts,
And contemplate Your ways.
I will delight myself in Your statutes;
I will not forget Your word.

Psalm 119:15–16

Let the word of Christ dwell in you richly in all wisdom, teaching and admonishing one another in psalms and hymns and spiritual songs, singing with grace in your hearts to the Lord.

Colossians 3:16

Those who wait on the LORD
Shall renew their strength;
They shall mount up with wings
    like eagles,
They shall run and not be weary,
They shall walk and not faint.

Isaiah 40:31

Draw near to God and He will draw near to you. Cleanse your hands, you sinners; and purify your hearts, you double-minded.

James 4:8

But put on the Lord Jesus Christ, and make no provision for the flesh, to fulfill its lusts.

Romans 13:14

Now by this we know that we know Him, if we keep His commandments.

He who says, "I know Him," and does not keep His commandments, is a liar, and the truth is not in him.

But whoever keeps His word, truly the love of God is perfected in him. By this we know that we are in Him.

He who says he abides in Him ought himself also to walk just as He walked.

1 John 2:3–6

In Him we live and move and have our being, as also some of your own poets have said, "For we are also His offspring."

Acts 17:28

Blessed is the man who listens to me,
Watching daily at my gates,
Waiting at the posts of my doors.

Proverbs 8:34

As newborn babes, desire the pure milk of the word, that you may grow thereby.

1 Peter 2:2

But be doers of the word, and not hearers only, deceiving yourselves.

James 1:22

Building Your Faith ✄

Now faith is the substance of things hoped for, the evidence of things not seen.

By faith we understand that the worlds were framed by the word of God, so that the things which are seen were not made of things which are visible.

But without faith it is impossible to please Him, for he who comes to God must believe that He is, and that He is a rewarder of those who diligently seek Him.

By faith he forsook Egypt, not fearing the wrath of the king; for he endured as seeing Him who is invisible.

Hebrews 11:1, 3, 6, 27

That the genuineness of your faith, being much more precious than gold that perishes, though it is tested by fire, may be found to praise, honor, and glory at the revelation of Jesus Christ, whom having not seen you love. Though now you do not see Him, yet believing, you rejoice with joy inexpressible and full of glory, receiving the end of your faith—the salvation of your souls.

1 Peter 1:7–9

For with God nothing will be impossible.

Luke 1:37

For in it the righteousness of God is revealed from faith to faith; as it is written, "The just shall live by faith."

Romans 1:17

So then faith comes by hearing, and hearing by the word of God.

Romans 10:17

Have I not commanded you? Be strong and of good courage; do not be afraid, nor be dismayed, for the LORD your God is with you wherever you go.

Joshua 1:9

If any of you lacks wisdom, let him ask of God, who gives to all liberally and without reproach, and it will be given to him.

But let him ask in faith, with no doubting, for he who doubts is like a wave of the sea driven and tossed by the wind.

For let not that man suppose that he will receive anything from the Lord; he is a double-minded man, unstable in all his ways.

James 1:5–8

He did not waver at the promise of God through unbelief, but was strengthened in faith, giving glory to God, and being fully convinced that what He had promised He was also able to perform.

Romans 4:20–21

We are hard pressed on every side, yet not crushed; we are perplexed, but not in despair; persecuted, but not forsaken; struck down, but not destroyed—always carrying about in the body the dying of the Lord Jesus, that the life of Jesus also may be manifested in our body.

2 Corinthians 4:8–10

What then shall we say to these things? If God is for us, who can be against us?

Romans 8:31

But you, beloved, building yourselves up on your most holy faith, praying in the Holy Spirit, keep yourselves in the love of God, looking for the mercy of our Lord Jesus Christ unto eternal life.

Jude 20, 21

We walk by faith, not by sight.

2 Corinthians 5:7

God's Plan of
Salvation . . .

God's Plan of Salvation ✈

For all have sinned and fall short of the glory of God.

Romans 3:23

But God demonstrates His own love toward us, in that while we were still sinners, Christ died for us.

Romans 5:8

Therefore, just as through one man sin entered the world, and death through sin, and thus death spread to all men, because all sinned.

Romans 5:12

For the wages of sin is death, but the gift of God is eternal life in Christ Jesus our Lord.

Romans 6:23

For God did not send His Son into the world to condemn the world, but that the world through Him might be saved.

John 3:17

He who believes in the Son has everlasting life; and he who does not believe the Son shall not see life, but the wrath of God abides on him.

John 3:36

Moreover, brethren, I declare to you the gospel which I preached to you, which also you received and in which you stand, by which also you are saved, if you hold fast that word which I preached to you—unless you believed in vain.

For I delivered to you first of all that which I also received: that Christ died for our sins according to the Scriptures, and that He was buried, and that He rose again the third day according to the Scriptures.

1 Corinthians 15:1–4

But as many as received Him, to them He gave the right to become children of God, to those who believe in His name.

John 1:12

For God so loved the world that He gave His only begotten Son, that whoever believes in Him should not perish but have everlasting life.

John 3:16

For by grace you have been saved through faith, and that not of yourselves; it is the gift of God, not of works, lest anyone should boast.

Ephesians 2:8, 9

Behold, I stand at the door and knock. If anyone hears My voice and opens the door, I will come in to him and dine with him, and he with Me.

Revelation 3:20

But what does it say? "The word is near you, in your mouth and in your heart" (that is, the word of faith which we preach): that if you confess with your mouth the Lord Jesus and believe in your heart that God has raised Him from the dead, you will be saved.

For with the heart one believes unto righteousness, and with the mouth confession is made unto salvation.

Romans 10:8–10

Therefore whoever confesses Me before men, him I will also confess before My Father who is in heaven.

Matthew 10:32

Let us hold fast the confession of our hope without wavering, for He who promised is faithful.

Hebrews 10:23

And this is the testimony: that God has given us eternal life, and this life is in His Son.

He who has the Son has life; he who does not have the Son of God does not have life.

These things I have written to you who believe in the name of the Son of God, that you may know that you have eternal life, and that you may continue to believe in the name of the Son of God.

1 John 5:11–13

How much better to get wisdom than gold!
And to get understanding is to be chosen
    rather than silver.
The highway of the upright is to depart
    from evil;
He who keeps his way preserves his soul.
Proverbs 16:16–17

PRAYER JOURNAL

_____
_____
_____
_____
_____
_____
_____
_____
_____
_____
_____
_____
_____
_____
_____
_____
_____
_____
_____
_____
_____
_____
_____
_____

NOTES

PRAYER JOURNAL

_____

_____

_____

_____

_____

_____

_____

_____

_____

_____

_____

_____

_____

_____

_____

_____

_____

_____

_____

_____

_____

_____

_____

_____

NOTES